It All Started With a Deli

THE ATTMANS OF LOMBARD STREET

A Remarkable Story of Business
and Family Success

M. Hirsh Goldberg

Apprentice House
Loyola University Maryland
Baltimore, Maryland

First Edition
Printed in the United States of America
Paperback ISBN: 978-1-934074-94-7
Ebook ISBN: 978-1-934074-31-2

Cover design by: Chelsea McGuckin
Internal design by: Chelsea McGuckin & Carlos Palacios

Cover Photo: Harry Attman, far right, behind the counter at his delicatessen, with his son Seymour, second from left, and two unidentified employees. Not shown: sons Edward and Leonard.

Published by Apprentice House

Apprentice House
Loyola University Maryland
4501 N. Charles Street
Baltimore, MD 21210
410.617.5265 •410.617.2198 (fax)
www.ApprenticeHouse.com
info@ApprenticeHouse.com

"Massachusetts has its Kennedys. Maryland has its Attmans. This family has created an impressive dynasty."

— Rabbi Stuart Weinblatt at Leonard and Phyllis Attman's annual Chanukah party co-hosted with Maryland's Governor in his official residence

"Attman's Delicatessen, now in its 95th year, is a Baltimore institution."

— *Baltimore Business Journal,* April, 2010

To The Memory of
Ida and Harry Attman
for the example they set
and the values they instilled
of hard work, charity, and
concern for others
as seen in this history of
five generations of Attmans

&

To My Wife, Gail,
with love and appreciation
for her valued assistance
in the preparation
of this book

CONTENTS

FOREWORD

by Martin O'Malley
Governor of Maryland

It is rare, even in a great City like Baltimore, for a business to survive for 100 years. Yet, Attman's Delicatessen is run by a very rare and special family. Few families have contributed so much to our City and State over these past four generations than the Attman family.

The story of the Attmans of Lombard Street and the famed Attman's Delicatessen is a fascinating one, and "It All Started With a Deli" captures the many facets of this intriguing tale.

I have had the privilege of being friends with many of the Attmans for many years. During my time serving as Mayor of Baltimore, I had the opportunity to officially name a street near Attman's Deli in memory of Seymour Attman soon after his untimely passing. Seymour was one of the three sons, along with Edward and Leonard, of Harry and Ida Attman, the founders and operators of Attman's Delicatessen.

Every year, Leonard Attman and his wife, Phyllis, and the extended Attman family are joint hosts with me and my wife for Chanukah parties in Government House.

In my time in Annapolis, Leonard has generously agreed to serve on the Maryland Stadium Authority, and Edward's son Gary has agreed to serve on the University of Maryland Board of Regents.

As you will see in these pages, Harry and Ida Attman, starting married life as poor immigrants, operated a small deli that would eventually garner a national mouth-watering reputation. It has now thrived close to a century.

Harry and Ida raised three sons and instilled them with the importance of education and the values of hard work, charity, faith, and giving back to the community. Those sons and their progeny would go on to build successful businesses that now employ thousands of people and serve the needs of a gamut of institutions, corporations, small and mid-size operations, and nonprofits. Their charitable endeavors help fund schools, hospitals, synagogues, non-denominational institutions, poverty programs, youth groups, and many other services touching many lives, here and abroad.

Indeed, the Attman story is one worth telling and sharing. It reminds us of what America can be for those who can seize its opportunities.

Chapter One

LUNCHTIME ON
LOMBARD STREET

Selling is like shaving. If you don't do it every day, you're a bum.

— Harry Attman

"Next!" It is midday at Attman's Delicatessen on Lombard Street in East Baltimore.

"Next!"

One after another, customers, squeezed into a narrow space the length of the store, call out their lunch orders as they pass single-file before a counter and display case filled with various deli meats. Amid the din, five employees work quickly behind the counter preparing and serving sandwiches and platters.

Today is a bright but cool day in 2009 more than 94 years and four generations of Attmans since 23-year-old Harry opened in 1915 a small shop selling confections and deli sandwiches, joined soon by his young bride Ida in 1918. The store is now becoming so crowded that the line soon doubles back on itself and eventually spills onto the sidewalk.

"Next! What'll you have?" a tall, burly counterman calls to the person now first in line, a middle-aged man in a business suit. Among those waiting in line behind him are laborers in jeans, two young nattily-dressed women, an elderly couple, college-age students, several more business or lawyer types, and a mixture of whites, blacks, Hispanics, Asians—all waiting for their deli fix.

Upon entering Attman's, patrons encounter a special atmosphere, not only the pungent aroma of delicatessen with its own salivating mix of steaming corned beef, hot pastrami, grilling hot dogs, spicy mustard, and savory pickles in brine. Customers also are enwrapped in the comforting sounds of friendly personnel bantering among themselves and with patrons. Plus there is the innovative humorous way the menu is featured here. The walls are filled with red, blue and white hand-lettered signs that tout such sandwiches as Tongue Fu, A Brisket A Basket, Hazza-Rye, the Gay Liveration, Ali and Tina Tuna, Turkey in the Straw, Lox O'Luck, and Cloak & Dagger (corned beef, coleslaw and of course Russian dressing).

Some sandwiches have hidden references in their names to Attman family members, such as Jessica Special, Ava Sampler, Stu's Kugel, Sara's Dagger, Jillian's Dessert, Ida's Jewish Apple Cake and Seymour's Original Fried Chicken.

All in all, patrons of Attman's can choose from 29 sandwiches, 32 combination sandwiches, 15 appetizers, 15 desserts and seven catering trays.

The quirky nature of the store can also be seen in its Kibbitz Room. To relieve the overcrowding in the original narrow store, Seymour Attman, second of three sons of the founders who took over managing the delicatessen when his father, Harry, died in 1968, bought the structure next door in 1970 and broke through the wall to create an area for tables and chairs. Until then, patrons had only a counter, opposite the display case, at which to stand to eat their sandwiches onsite. When Seymour passed away in 2002, his son, Marc, took over and maximized what Seymour had started.

The walls of the Kibbitz Room are now filled with photos, articles, and reviews, showing the wide popularity of Attman's and the Attman family. Here we see a photograph of Jimmy Carter sampling an Attman's hot dog during Carter's campaign for president. Here, too, are pictures of Seymour and his brothers Edward and Leonard with Presidents Bill Clinton, Lyndon Johnson, and Ronald Reagan; with Maryland Governors Mandel, Glendenning, Ehrlich, and O'Malley;

and with Teddy Kennedy and Henry Kissinger.

Also posted are framed citations from *Southern Living* and *City Paper* naming Attman's Baltimore's Best Deli, a Zagat Survey Award of Distinction, and a Maryland Restaurant Association Medal of Honor.

The American delis may have started in New York City, but Attman's—cited in the book Great American Delis as one of a select group of delis in the nation and the only one from Baltimore— refers, in its cheeky way, in its menu as offering "authentic New York delicatessen (only better)."

An insight into why Attman's Delicatessen has survived and prospered so long can be found in the sentiments left in the Guest Book set up in the Kibbitz Room for patrons to sign. A selection:

"I was born and bred in Baltimore, but I'm now in Atlanta. I drove 12 hours just to eat this bit of heaven. Excellent!"

"We came from Rhode Island in search of the best pastrami sandwich. Mission accomplished!"

"We're Red Sox season ticket holders. Wish we had a deli this good near Fenway!"

"This is our 35th wedding anniversary, and where did we choose to eat, but with you! We used to eat here in the 1970s when we lived in D.C. So nice to travel back to you today to celebrate our special day." — New Canaan, Connecticut

"I was born in New York and moved to Baltimore in 1966. When I feel nostalgia for the lower East Side of NYC and the 'old' Baltimore, I come here. Corned beef (hot) on rye with mustard is food for the inner woman. Keep the tradition going."

"All the way from Prague, Czech Republic, Europe. Now living in Towson. Best deli ever. Long live Attman's. J"

On the street outside Attman's, however, there are few other indications of when this section of Lombard Street, in the early to mid-1900s, was a thriving center for immigrant Jewish life and a shopping mecca for Jews and others in Baltimore. In a two-block area decades ago, small family-owned and operated shops were selling baked goods, groceries, dairy products, meats, fish, fruits, vegetables, candy, horseradish, hardware, clothing, pots and pans, imported foods, even live chickens, and of course deli. The narrow first-floor shops in what had been three-story row houses were usually so stocked with goods that merchants often displayed their wares on the sidewalk, in bins or barrels, the merchandise even hanging from poles. Black-and-white photos of the day show Lombard Street crowded with automobiles and delivery trucks and shoppers.

All of this is gone. Attman's is now bordered by a paved parking lot on one side and a vacant lot on the other. Across the street a chain link fence encloses an open, bare space. None of the original structures remain, except Attman's.

But the interest and nostalgia for that period remain. A block away, in the middle of Lloyd Street near Lombard, the Jewish Museum of Maryland, situated between two restored synagogues built in the1800s, is on this day featuring a major exhibition on the Lombard Street area in its heyday.

A prominent part of the show is a segment on 'Corned Beef Row,' with special attention to Attman's Delicatessen and its Kibbitz Room. When after 2½ years of development, the museum on October 14, 2007, unveiled "Voices of Lombard Street: A Century of Change in East Baltimore," the exhibit met with such a large turnout at the opening that the museum's executive director, Avi Decter, termed the scene a "sardine can" of people.

"That day was also opening day for the Baltimore Ravens and we were petrified no one would attend, but we had the first or second largest crowd ever," he recalled in an interview I had with him. The show has remained popular ever since, and Decter said that plans are to retain it for "five to ten years and maintain it as our 'core' exhibit." This would be the first time that the Jewish Museum of Maryland kept a show for such an extended time.

To mount "Voices of Lombard Street," Decter related that because Lombard Street is so well-known for its food, the museum sought and received key financial help from several families associated with food and Lombard Street. One of those families was the Attmans, and exhibit materials prominently list major gifts from the descendants of Harry and Ida: the Edward and Mildred Attman Family, the Leonard and Phyllis Attman Family, and the Seymour Attman Family.

"The Attmans could not make the opening, so we hosted a special brunch reception for them the following Sunday. Four generations of Attmans came and toured the exhibit, with the older group answering questions from the younger ones about what it was like back then," Decter said.

"We love the Attmans. They are wonderful neighbors. Marc Attman has supported our speaker series for several years, covering the costs for marketing and sending out speakers. And the family as a whole has been encouraging for years. These are people who not only get with you, but stay with you."

Decter remembers Harry Attman fondly. "Harry was a doll. He was a sweetie. I'm sure he was a tough-minded businessman, because you can't run a deli in the midst of competing delis and succeed like he did. I remember him as hustling around. He was very active, not a passive manager. He was always there and everybody knew it. He must have been a ball of fire in his youth."

It is an interesting observation. At one time, seven delicatessens competed for business on Lombard Street. Today, only two other Lombard Street delis besides Attman's exist, one of which is open for limited hours and the other is slated to give way to an expansion of the Jewish Museum. Only Attman's remains, with its original vigor and its reputation, as a one-of-a-kind destination delicatessen that is not just intact, but still growing.

But the presence of Attman's Delicatessen today has an additional story to tell: how the children and grandchildren and, in fact, now the great-grandchildren of Harry and Ida Attman have built other successful enterprises and careers as well. And they have accomplished these successes by learning from and employing many of the business and ethical principles Harry and Ida practiced and taught.

This unusual and compelling story can be said to start with a pair of scissors.

Chapter Two
WHEN HARRY MET IDA

My grandmother taught us how to live.
My grandfather taught us how to work.

— Steven Attman

Between 1880 and 1924 when U.S. immigration laws became highly restrictive, 24 million immigrants of various nationalities streamed into the United Sates. Of those, an estimated 2.2 million were Jewish, most of them from Eastern Europe, in what has been termed the third wave of Jewish immigration to America. This wave dwarfed the first wave, of Spanish or Sephardic Jews from 1640 to 1820, and the second, of German Jews, from 1820 to 1880. In the case of Eastern European Jews, they were not only "yearning to breathe free," but fleeing from gathering threats to their safety. Among those millions were two families: the Gettmans (the original name of the Attmans in Europe) and the Shapiros who came at different times in different ways during those years, but all of whom eventually settled in Baltimore, Maryland and gave rise to this family's history.

The mass of Jewish people who lived through those times witnessed years of great turmoil. With the emancipation of Western Europe's Jewry in the 19th century, Jews were beginning to enter into general society. But Eastern Europe itself was undergoing seismic changes in their governments and society. In the past, social and economic upheaval often led to the implementation of anti-Jewish policies and physical attacks on Jews as the general populace looked for reasons for their woes, and lashed out at scapegoats in their midst. In Russia, for instance, in 1881, revolutionaries assassinated Czar Alexander II. The death of this czar, an advocate of many anti-Semitic policies, only led to more social unrest and to the next czar who was even more anti-Semitic. Anti-Semitism was ever present, either in the form of discriminatory government policies or in peasant-inspired destructive, deadly pogroms that swept periodically through Jewish shtetls and villages in Russia, Poland, Lithuania, and the Ukraine. The years leading up to the eruption of World War I in 1914 and in the war's aftermath proved to be a time of additional troubles for the Jews. Through all this, America beckoned as a welcoming haven of acceptance for Jews, spurring many to leave their homes in Europe and seek new lives in America.

Troubled by the ever-constant threat of pogroms, the dire economic times, and the restrictions on employment and religious practices, Harry Attman's parents urged him to go to America. It was the general practice among Jews for one family member to travel to the United States, find work and, it was hoped, save enough money to help bring other family members over. And so in November 1912, 20-year-old Harry Attman became the first in his family to emigrate to America.

Harry (his Hebrew name was Tzvi) was born in Kusmien, Russia, a village near the Polish border, on October 26, 1893, to Shmarja and Sluva Gettman (in English their names became Shmariah and Sylvia). Shmarja was a grain dealer. The eldest of nine children, Harry had three brothers and five sisters (two of whom were born after he left home). In one of many sacrifices he would make for his family, Harry, by traveling alone to America, would not see his parents, brothers and sisters for eleven years.

Small but athletic and solidly built, Harry was adventuresome and looked forward to his new life. He first traveled from his home to the port city of Rotterdam where he boarded the ship *Uranium* for voyage across the Atlantic Ocean. It was just several months after the *Titanic* had sunk in the Atlantic after hitting an iceberg on its maiden voyage. Joining the crowded third class passenger area far below deck, he carried with his meager possessions an unusual set of implements for him: a pair of scissors, a razor, and a comb with which he planned to cut hair. It was one of the first indications of his enterprising spirit that would eventually find full display in his own business. While America at that time was a welcoming country to immigrants, government authorities were also careful to screen passengers for diseases and other problems before allowing anyone to disembark. Those who looked sickly or exhibited any of a series of disabilities faced the prospect of being sent back to their country of origin. In a Special Notice to Passengers given out at entry points and kept thereafter by Harry among his papers, the following warning was issued:

> *No person who is Insane, Imbecile, Deaf, Dumb,*
> *Blind, Crippled or otherwise infirm or suffering from*
> *Trachoma, Tuberculosis, Favus, or any other contagious*
> *disease will be permitted to land, nor any person*
> *without money or baggage, or in any way liable to*
> *become a public charge, nor any person who has been an*
> *inmate of a prison, poor-house or work-house or any*
> *charitable institution.*

Only those who passed scrutiny were allowed into the United States. Others were sent back, even if it meant breaking-up families. The lucky ones admitted into the country often found immigrant officials marking on their clothing an "OK" in chalk.

Harry used his set of scissors/razor/comb to earn money by charging for his services as a barber for his fellow travelers, but he was also helping them avoid those dreaded problems with inspection. In those days, a transatlantic voyage could take two weeks or more. The rough Atlantic seas could make the trip difficult, especially for the third class passengers below deck where most of the immigrants booked the cheapest passage. In fact, one young passenger who came across at about the same time as Harry later remembered how many of the passengers became violently seasick. Harry's barber services must have seemed appealing to those who wished to look healthy and their children well-cared-for when they disembarked and had to pass the scrutiny of U.S. officials.

Young Harry was showing how he instinctively grasped what the author of one of the most successful business books of that and future eras advocated. Napoleon Hill, born into poverty in America in 1883 ten years before Harry was born and living through the same time period as Harry, advised individuals in *Think and Grow Rich* that the road to business success in the America of the time (and at any time thereafter) was to "find a need and fill it." Harry had sensed a need on that voyage and filled it. He and later his sons exhibited this entrepreneurial spirit and implemented such a strategy as they each built highly successful enterprises. Interestingly, family members cannot recall any time that Harry, before or after that voyage to America, ever picked up scissors and gave anyone a haircut.

When Harry arrived at Ellis Island on November 23, 1912, he experienced the first change in his life in the New World. Immigration agents gave him a new name. At birth, he was named Harry Gettman, but after passing through the immigration process he found that his last name was printed out on documents as Ettman, which was later transcribed as Attman. Such a name-change was not an uncommon experience for immigrants. Many of these officials could not understand the language or read the writing of immigrants. In the processing of hundreds if not thousands of people a day, many speaking Yiddish, Polish, German, or Russian, officials often recorded names in variant English. 'Gettman' may have sounded or looked like 'Ettman' and so Harry Gettman of Russia eventually became Harry Attman in America. [A similar name change occurred to another immigrant to Baltimore who eventually entered the food business. A kosher caterer named Baida, who operated in Baltimore in the latter half of the 1900s, was given that name after he followed his brother through the immigration line; when asked his last name, he replied in Yiddish, *"Baida dazelba,"* which means "the same as his." He subsequently found on his papers that his last name in English was now Baida.]

After being admitted into the United States, Harry traveled to Providence, Rhode Island, where a cousin on his mother's side, Harry Mittelman, lived and operated a deli/confectionery store. This was Harry's first introduction to employment in the food business. He worked in the store for several years, was paid $5 a week, and lived upstairs. By 1915, Harry was ready for a change. He went to Baltimore to meet some friends, liked the city, which was experiencing a rapidly growing Jewish community from the influx of immigrants coming through the city's port, and decided to stay. It was in Baltimore that he met his future wife, Ida.

Ida (Chaya Feiga) Shapiro was born on May 17, 1900, in the town of Podwoloscycka, Poland, near the Russian border. She was the oldest of six children born to Yechiel Eliyahu and Rachael Leah Shapiro. Like Harry, Ida was the first of her family to come to

America, arriving at the age of 15. She went directly to Baltimore where she had an aunt living on Aisquith Street and stayed with her while working for the Sonnenborn Company as a seamstress. When she and Harry met at a social gathering for young Jewish adults who had recently arrived in the U.S., they felt an immediate and as it turned out a lasting attraction. They made a striking couple who shared many compatible traits and they soon planned to marry.

As we will come to see, both Harry and Ida possessed the emotional warmth, the entrepreneurial spirit and a wide range of abilities that would prove key to their accomplishments and those of the progeny that would issue from their marriage. Harry came to be known by customers and community for being friendly, with a good sense of humor. He was a well-rounded person: hardworking, earnest and religious, as well as an adept dancer and swimmer. He could speak five languages fluently: Russian, Polish, Italian, Yiddish and English. Although all-business at work, he was a strong family person. His first grandchild, Ronald, fondly remembers how when he graduated college, his grandfather, who had never attended college, presented him with a generous gift and wept with emotion.

Ida was also a people-person and outgoing and, like Harry, very charitable. Their son Edward often cites her sharp mind and her unerring business and personal advice that proved to set him, correctly, on a life-long career. Their second child, Seymour, found her to be a very loving mother. Leonard, another son, remembers her as being "a tall and stately woman of regal bearing in both her manner and dress." She also became known as an excellent cook and baker. "Nothing is as good as her strudel," remembers her grandson, Gary; and another grandchild, Shellye, proudly reprinted in her synagogue's cookbook one of Ida's 'secret' recipes, "Bubby Attman's Chocolate Chip Honey Cake," a dessert that she would bake every Jewish New Year and is still offered in the Attman delicatessen. She was so adept at sewing it was said she could look at an advertisement for a dress and make it in a day. But above all, it would be her sense of family, her close and supportive relationship with her husband and children that would help guide them all to success. "She imbued the family with a sense of destiny," said Gary.

Harry and Ida married on October 25, 1918. The ceremony was performed by Rabbi Abraham N. Schwartz, a leading figure in Baltimore's religious Jewish community who in 1917 had founded the Talmudical Academy of Baltimore, the first Hebrew day school to be launched in the United States outside New York City. Harry and Ida would later enroll their children in this school for all or part of their Jewish education.

Harry and Ida's marriage came during a major health crisis in America and throughout the world. The Spanish Flu, first confirmed in a soldier at a military camp in Kansas in March of 1918, had become pandemic by August. During the ensuing year, the Spanish Flu killed 600,000 people in the United States and 25 million people worldwide (twice the number of people killed during World War I). Although public health restrictions were put into place to halt the illness, daily life continued for most people and the couple pressed ahead with their wedding plans.

Once married, Harry and Ida began jointly operating a small confectionery/deli that Harry had started in 1915 on the corner of 2000 East Baltimore and Washington Streets, not far from Lombard Street. Here, while selling candies and sodas and other confections,

Harry had also started selling salami and bologna sandwiches for a nickel to people on their way to work or at night to youths hanging out in the neighborhood. The new couple worked closely together to make this business successful, living in rooms in the back of the store, renting out rooms on the second and third floors and, in what became characteristic of their working lives, putting in long hours. They soon teamed up with a partner to buy a store from Nathan and Elsie Weinstein at 1019 East Lombard Street, where they opened a food market and deli. Harry and Ida operated stores in both locations until 1927, when they decided to concentrate on their Lombard Street location and closed their first store. They took full ownership of the delicatessen in 1940 when the partnership dissolved. But Harry and Ida continued to live at 2000 East Baltimore Street while rearing three sons: Edward born in 1920, Seymour in 1927, and Leonard in 1934, eventually moving to a home in Colonial Village in Northwest Baltimore in 1953.

During their early years in Baltimore and in spite of the pressures of building a business and starting to raise a family, Harry and Ida worked to fulfill a promised goal: to bring their families to America.

First, they brought over Ida's family in 1920. On February 24, 1920, in an affidavit required by U.S. immigration authorities, Harry swore that he was "willing, able and ready to purchase steamship tickets for his said mother-in-law and family to come and live with him...and that he is willing and able to receive, maintain, and support the aforesaid immigrants." At that time, Ida's mother was 48 and a widow (her husband and a son had been murdered during a pogrom the year before) and the children that came with her were Enda, 19; Dolora, 16; Rose, 14; and, Jacob, 13.

Later, on August 7, 1923, after much planning and correspondence, Harry brought his father, mother and siblings to America. More than two years before, in February of 1921, Harry had prepaid $1471.16 for their intended passage from Hamburg to New York by boat and then by train to Baltimore. This sum was to cover $1125 for third class passage on a Swedish American Line steamship (the s/s Drottningholm) for his father, mother, six adult siblings (Rachel, Joseph, Golda, Abraham, Feiga and Schloima) and two young sisters (Chaika, 9, and Anna, 6), plus a U.S. head tax of $56, railway fare of $65.16 and landing money of $225. When a problem arose in their processing through Immigration in 1923, Harry traveled to New York and to Ellis Island to appear as a witness in their behalf before the Board of Special Inquiry (U.S. Immigration Law required that "every alien who is not clearly and beyond a doubt entitled to land" had to appear before this body).

To make the trip and stay over, Harry took a room at the Broadway Central Hotel in New York City (the hotel touted itself as offering "accommodations better than indicated by the moderate rates charged"). While at the hotel, Harry wrote Ida a nine-page letter in Yiddish on the hotel stationery to keep her apprised of developments. He told her of how distressed he was at seeing the conditions in which the newly-arrived immigrants were waiting to be processed ("things are so crowded you can't even put a pin") and bemoaned what his family had experienced before and during the trip ("so many tribulations they have had to endure"). With a reference to *Hashem* on every page, he declared however that "one has to be strong and trust." In an indication of their closeness, Harry also included an endearing message: "I kiss you my dear sweet pearl." [Note: This letter, along with numerous letters and postcards in Yiddish that Harry's family had sent to him from Europe, were saved over the years in a metal Salome Mild Havana Smoker cigar box that Harry, then Seymour, and then his son, Marc, kept.]

To expend all this effort and provide $1400 in funding was quite remarkable for anyone to undertake, especially in those days for a person operating a small business. As indicated in his Affidavit of Support that the government required, Harry, who at the time had a wife and one child and was "engaged in delicatessen and grocery business," was earning $2500 a year. To help pay for the transportation expenses for his family, Harry also took out a loan that he then repaid over coming years.

The fact that Harry and Ida were able to bring their families to America by the end of 1923 is significant because the next year, due to the political pressures building against the growing influx of immigrants, the U.S. immigration laws were dramatically changed, essentially closing America's fabled golden doors to Catholics and Jews from Eastern and Southern Europe.

Together, Harry and Ida eventually were able to facilitate the emigration to the United States of three of their parents, as well as brothers, sisters, and other family members: a total of 19 relatives.

But they were unable to bring two members of Ida's family to the safety of America. On the holiday of Shavuot on June 4, 1919, after they had arranged for their passports and were just months away from leaving, Ida's father and a brother, who had served in the Russian army, were both shot and killed during a pogrom. Shaken by this, Harry and Ida would later name two of their children in memory of Ida's father and brother.

Without the efforts of Harry and Ida, the Attman and Shapiro family lines would undoubtedly not have survived the violence that swept through their towns in Europe during the coming two decades. Both areas were overrun by the Nazis and engulfed in the Holocaust. It is estimated that of the Jewish population of 3.3 million alive in Poland at the start of World War II, only 369,000 Jews—11 percent—survived.

Meanwhile, in Baltimore, Harry and Ida were creating a family that would not only survive, but flourish over four generations and into the 21st century.

Chapter Three

BUILDING A BUSINESS, RAISING A FAMILY

"We're proud of our heritage.
We're proud of our family members.
That means a lot to us."

— Marc Attman

When Harry and Ida started their married life in 1918, Baltimore City was a tapestry of burgeoning ethnic communities, the third most populated city in the country. Baltimore was then such a prominent force in America that the current President of the United States, Woodrow Wilson, had been nominated for the presidency in Baltimore's Fifth Regiment Armory, then the ninth presidential convention Baltimore had hosted. Only New York City and Philadelphia had more population. Baltimore's prominence was due in large part to its being both a major East Coast shipping port and the hub for the B&O Railroad, America's first railway system.

As a port city, it became America's second leading entry point for the thousands of immigrants arriving by ship. The city's processing center for new immigrants at Locust Point, situated near Fort McHenry, rivaled New York's Ellis Island for size and significance. Many immigrants—non-Jews arriving from Europe and the Mediterranean, as well as Jews from Eastern and Western Europe—settled into the city's burgeoning immigrant communities that preceded them. Another segment in the increasingly diverse ethnic populace was a small but growing black population as they moved away from oppressive Southern states, entered Maryland on their way north, and stayed. In fact, a contingent of black families lived in several narrow streets radiating from the Jewish area of Lombard Street.

However, Baltimore was also becoming one of the most segregated of American cities. Some of this was by personal preference, as Jews often chose to live among co-religionists, and Germans, Irish, Polish,

Greek and Italians eagerly formed their own neighborhoods. Little Italy persists today as a reminder of that era. But African-Americans found themselves restricted to living in certain areas of the city, first by unwritten but openly known segregated 'redlining' directives and then by formally legislated codes. Jews, too, faced restrictive neighborhood covenants that prevented them from buying homes in various high-end communities, such as Roland Park and Guilford. The result of both informal and formal segregation was that the various blocks around Lombard Street in East Baltimore were, for practical reasons, associated with religious, ethnic or racial communities that grouped themselves together. By the 1950s, restrictive covenants were ruled unconstitutional, and Jews and blacks could more easily live throughout metropolitan Baltimore. Such changes helped speed up the move by Jews away from East Baltimore, such that Lombard Street was no longer a magnet for attracting shoppers to Jewish-owned stores.

Attman's Delicatessen survived these population shifts. One explanation for its continued presence on Lombard Street is that Harry and Ida and later their family conducted their business in a way that reached out to everyone, not only to Jews but also to non-Jews, whites and blacks, those of high social status and the poor. As a result, many Baltimoreans still have fond memories of the couple and of Attman's Delicatessen, and have remained friends and patrons. Among those is Maryland State Senator Nathanial McFadden, a leader of the state's black legislators and now chairman of the Baltimore City Senate Delegation: the Attmans gave him his first job as a youngster working in the deli, an experience he tells others he has treasured; he also recounts how they also encouraged him to get a college education and pursue a career. In fact, the Attmans' relationship with African Americans may have ensured the delicatessen's survival. During the Baltimore riots in 1968 in the aftermath of the assassination of Martin Luther King, Jr., blacks living in the neighborhood only let fire trucks into the area when flames threatened the Attman's store so that it could escape the fires consuming many other shops along Lombard Street.

How did Harry and Ida build a small delicatessen into a Baltimore food icon that has survived and thrived for nearly a century? After all, few if any companies or organizations endure for 100 years. And the Attmans have accomplished this in the face of hard times, both on personal and national levels. They had to deal with the disruption of a world war, a major pandemic (the worldwide Spanish influenza of 1918 struck the city particularly hard, with Baltimore experiencing the fourth highest death rate among U.S. cities), the Great Depression (during which the delicatessen almost went bankrupt, numerous periodic economic downturns, a race riot, prolonged traffic obstructions, road closings, changing neighborhoods, family deaths, all while rearing three children: Edward (born May 31, 1920), Seymour (April 27, 1926), and Leonard (February 18, 1934).

They also attempted to join with two other partners intending to launch a chain of food markets with deli departments. The partners opened one of these stores on Garrison Boulevard near Belvedere Avenue. When that store was not successful, Harry and Ida bought the 1019 East Lombard Street location from the partner who owned the building.

Consider, too, that Harry and Ida suffered from the shady dealings of a partner they took into their business when they bought the store on Lombard Street. Harry renamed the business A & L Delicatessen to incorporate the initials of their two last names. When he eventually discovered that "L," who opened the store in the morning, had been stealing cash from the register, Harry confronted him. Caught red-handed, a red-faced "L" immediately left and never returned.

So how did Harry and Ida accomplish so much and pass on to their children and grandchildren the lessons that led to the family's continued successes?

The first instruction was an attention to the products they sold. They offered good quality food and the better cuts of meat prepared with spices and seasonings in a special recipe Harry and Ida developed. That recipe has remained a secret, known by only a few Attman family members and the current manager. Some of Ida's recipes for baked goods are also still used. Harry purchased with an eye to keep costs down and to respond to changing tastes of customers. He would buy cucumbers at the height of the season in August and put them up as pickles in big barrels. The Attmans also put up their own tomatoes, storing them in cold storage until they were ready for sale. They imported herrings from Norway (for making pickled herring), Scotland (to make *matjes* herring), and Iceland (for schmaltz herring), and put them in cold storage for later sale, often selling several barrels of herring a day. They also sold, in bulk, dried lima beans, split peas, and a variety of grains.

In preparation for Passover, they featured 100-pound burlap bags of walnuts, hazel nuts, butternuts and almonds; barrels of kosher salamis and bolognas; and wooden cases of dried apricots, sweet and sour prunes, and various-size pears. To serve the Passover needs of Jewish customers in small towns, the Attmans distributed circulars throughout the South and shipped orders to them by American Railway Express. "I remember staying up at night after the store closed to fill these orders," says Ed. He also remembers the matzohs then in demand: Wittenberg Matzoh (the least expensive at 10 cents a pound), Manischewitz (12 to 13 cents per pound), Streit's, and Goodman's.

Another reason for their growing success was undoubtedly the couple's willingness to work together and work hard, adjusting always to the changing times and needs of their customers. The area around Lombard Street was initially filled with people struggling to integrate into American life. Jewish East Baltimore was crowded with the influx of thousands of destitute newcomers, many of whom spoke Yiddish and little or no English and had to contend with rearing children in a new world while the parents themselves emerged fitfully from the old. Jews tried to earn their livelihood as garment workers, seamstresses, tailors, laborers, hired hands, and tutors. Some of the more enterprising set up their own shops. Most families lived in crowded apartments with few amenities and limited sanitary conditions.

Innovations that made life easier came slowly over the next decades as Harry and Ida sought to bring up a family: the Attmans did not have an indoor bathroom with bathtub and hot water until 1927, when Edward was seven (until then, outhouses were common and communal bathhouses were the rule); instead of electric lights, dangerous gas jets illuminated homes at night; linoleum was yet to be introduced to cover bare floors; instead of refrigerators, insulated boxes were cooled with blocks of ice delivered by truck. In the summertime, to escape a hot, humid Baltimore night, the Attman children would take blankets and sleep in nearby Patterson Park. Still in the distant future were air conditioning, easy access to telephones, and affordable automobiles.

However, all these people, living in the same conditions and from the same religious and cultural backgrounds, found common ground and camaraderie. In the Jewish areas, the streets were alive with people of all ages, but especially young adults who had been the early arriving immigrants and the children of newly forming families. At one point, sixty synagogues dotted the area around Lombard Street. And seemingly at the center of it all was that crowded row of shops along several blocks of Lombard Street where patrons could find much of their needs for home: from live fish and chickens to two-cent chocolate sodas to clothing and hardware items.

Across the street from Attman's store was Blank's department store, which carried a variety of fabrics. Within the same block was Fayman's and Ben's, two stores which handled all kinds of clothing, from socks for children and bras for women to men's pants and shirts, much of it in odd lots. There was Brotman's kosher butcher shop, Yankelov's chickens, and down the street Lazinsky's fish store and Crystal's Bakery. Next door to Attman's was Holzman's Bakery. In the 1100 block of Lombard Street was Stone's Bakery, where patrons could buy hot rolls and bagels, baked fresh every hour. Among the other delis was Atlantic Import, operated by Harry's parents, brother, and brother-in-law. That store lasted until the riots.

As an Italian woman who grew up in nearby Little Italy told me about her memories of her mother taking her there to shop, "Thanks to those Jewish merchants, Lombard Street then was our supermarket before there were supermarkets."

For Jews living and working in the Lombard Street area, it was a competitive life combined with a closeness of family and community. This was especially true for Harry and Ida. Running a food-oriented business, and doing so in two locations—Baltimore Street and Lombard Street until 1946 when they sold the Baltimore street building—was challenging and demanding. They worked part or all of seven days a week, with their busiest days Thursday, Saturday night, and Sunday. "My father always said whenever he came into work it was too late, and whenever he left it was too early," Edward remembers. "And he never would pull the blind down and say, 'We're closed.' If a customer came and needed something, he opened up the store to take care of him. That was his nature to do that."

Leonard, too, remembers how his mother would delay dinner until his father would come home, which could be late because his father often stayed open to serve late-arriving customers. "When are we going to eat?" Leonard would ask, and his mother would reply, "When your father comes. When there's no more business, then he comes home." Although the family would always wait, Leonard found to his surprise that nothing ever seemed to get burned, that "everything seemed to taste good no matter what time we ate." Leonard also saw first-hand his father's work ethic and concern for others. When he worked in the store alongside his father, he remembered the times when even though they had already turned off the lights to go home, his father might see a car coming down Lombard Street and say, 'I can't close it up. These people may be coming from somewhere and need to get food.'

"And many times we would reopen the store, turn on all the lights and take care of these people."

That attention to customer service was a hallmark of Harry and Ida's attitude about business, and they conveyed it to their children. Marc Attman, Seymour's son, recalls Seymour relating to him the lessons he learned from his parents:

— "Always go out of your way to be a diplomat."

— "Look into a person's eyes when you talk to them."

— "When you say something, mean it."

As with many small family-owned businesses, the Attman children helped out in the store. Edward, being the oldest, was the first to help, working after school and on weekends. When he was old enough to reach the slicing machine, he cut deli on a hand-operated slicer before electric slicers were introduced. Even after he graduated high school and was attending University of Baltimore, Eddie would work every day after school because "things were very tough in those years" and he wanted to help pay for his college tuition (then costing $30 a month, an amount the Attmans strained to meet). He continued to help out for a while even after he returned from his army service following World War II. As they became older, Seymour and Leonard also worked in the store after school. It proved to be an important experience for their future business lives, as Leonard later acknowledged in an interview with the Jewish Museum of Maryland: "It gave me the ability, as well as my brothers, to get to meet people from all different ethnic backgrounds and be able to interact with anyone of any race, creed, color with a degree of ease, then as well as now."

As a 10-year-old, Leonard would at times be assigned to work the cash register and give change. Since Harry knew five languages fluently, he imparted this awareness to his children as a way to enhance customer relations and sales. "My father wanted the customer always to feel at home. So he made me learn taking cash and counting change back to them in their language. If people came in and they could only speak Yiddish, I was to count the money back to them in Yiddish. If they were Russian, I was to count back in Russian. To this day, I can still count extremely rapidly from one to 100 in Russian. I can also say in Russian 'hello,' 'you're welcome,' and 'thank you.'"

The result was a customer who was both astonished and appreciative.

"I made that person feel at home coming into the store," Leonard says. "And they would look forward to that. Here is this young kid who would be in their safety zone, so to speak, that somebody like that would be handling their money, giving them the cash. They didn't even always look at the money. They just looked at me counting it to them in their own language."

Seymour, too, learned some Yiddish, Russian and Italian as a way to further business, as he recounted in a 1982 oral history interview with the Jewish Historical Society of Maryland: "If you could speak the language, you could sell because a lot of people were immigrants, so you could suggest this or that to them, like a herring is a '*shlutke*,' and butter is '*matzlaw*,' which is Russian. In Jewish you would say '*pitter*' or '*putter*.' I had a lot of Russian people come in and this is the way I learned. They got a big kick out of this because they would think I was a foreigner. When they asked me where I was from and I would tell them I'm born in America, they would really crack up. It was a novelty for them. Just like it would be a novelty if you'd go to Europe and some child spoke English."

Later, some of Harry and Ida's grandchildren would come down to the store to help. Marc, Seymour's son who now manages the delicatessen, started as an 8-year-old assisting in the store. Ed's son, Ron, the oldest of the grandchildren and the first of his generation to work in the deli, would arrive on a Saturday night and work as cashier ("I could only make change in English," he recalls). Here he saw the array of patrons who would come by: both the poor who had only 25 cents for a bag of deli shavings, as well as judges, policemen, politicians, and community leaders. Even then-Maryland State Comptroller Louis Goldstein would frequent Attman's on Saturday nights. "I learned more about people those Saturday nights than I ever expected," Ron says.

Another aspect of Harry and Ida Attman that left a life-long imprint on their children was their charitableness, with both food and money. During the Depression or when it was hard times, Harry would provide 6 ounce bags of food to any homeless individual who came to the store. Collectors for Jewish charities would also visit the store for donations, and Harry never turned them away without some contribution. Harry would also often offer collectors a chance to sit down and have a roll and coffee, and then converse with them about politics, religion or Torah. According to Leonard, if there were a sickness in the family or any other problem, his father would mention the problem to these collectors, many of whom were rabbis, and they would declare they would go back and say an extra special prayer. True to their word, a letter would come back to Harry attesting that the prayers had been made. Later, these contacts proved helpful when Seymour needed an operation in Milwaukee and a rabbi from Milwaukee who had periodically visited the store for years put the family up for the week that they were in the city while Seymour underwent his operation.

Ida, too, was charitable. She was an active sponsor of the ladies auxiliaries in behalf of religious schools and donated to charities by means of *pushkes* (charity boxes) that she kept in the house. The sons remember her standard practice every Friday afternoon or on the eve of a Jewish holiday. Before she lit candles, she would open a closet door and put pennies, nickels, dimes or quarters—in multiples of 18 or 36 (representing in numbers the Hebrew word for "life")—into the 15 charity boxes that she had nailed to the back of the door. These charity boxes were from different schools, yeshivas or organizations located in Baltimore, New York, Cleveland, and other cities, as well as in Israel (then Palestine). Periodically, a collector would come by to collect the money and leave a receipt for the donations. Among those boxes was one from the synagogue in Milwaukee.

The Jewish religion and Jewish traditions were a central part of the Attman home and imbued Edward, Seymour and Leonard with meaningful and lasting impressions.

The Attmans kept a kosher home and observed all the Jewish holidays. On Friday night and Saturday after services, the family ate together, with Ida providing meals and desserts of her own recipes. Harry put on *tefillin* every weekday, and Ida prayed each morning from a prayer book especially geared for women. Called a *Techina*, the prayers were printed in Yiddish.

To Harry and Ida, the Jewish education of their children was, as Leonard says, "of prime importance."

For their Jewish education, Ed, Seymour and Leonard were enrolled in the Hebrew Parochial School (later to be named the Talmudical Academy of Baltimore; founded in 1917, it was the first Hebrew day school in America outside New York City). In its beginning years, the school held Hebrew classes in the morning and secular classes in the afternoon for boys until the 6ᵗʰ grade, with Hebrew classes offered from 3:30 to 5:30 pm for children who went to public school. Ed and Seymour went until the 6ᵗʰ grade, and then went to public school while continuing their Hebrew education in the school's afternoon classes. Being the youngest of the brothers, Leonard remained at the Talmudical Academy as the school eventually expanded its Hebrew and secular classes, adding a junior high and then a high school. At first, classes were taught in Yiddish since many of the teachers, themselves immigrants knowing little English, translated from the Hebrew into Yiddish. Later, instruction was in English and instructors of secular classes were both Jewish and non-Jewish, with many teachers experienced public school instructors. While Edward and Seymour went on to graduate from public high schools, Leonard graduated in one of Talmudical Academy's earliest 12ᵗʰ grades.

Says Leonard about his Jewish education, "That gave me the values that I live with today and probably have been the most help to me in my business, my social life and attaining what success I have been able to achieve."

The family belonged to Shomrei Mishmeres, an Orthodox synagogue now referred to as the Lloyd Street Shul, which was down the street from where the Jewish Museum of Maryland now stands. The building featured a balcony for the women worshippers and a downstairs mikvah, frequented at separate times by women and men. Before Passover, matzoh was baked on the basement level. All three Attman boys had their Bar Mitzvahs in this shul. Ida cooked and baked the food for the Bar Mitzvah kiddush held after Sabbath services in the synagogue's reception hall, making her own honey cake, mandel bread and chickpeas mixture (called *nahit*). As with most Bar Mitzvahs of the day, no additional parties or festivities were held, but Ida arranged for that Sunday for the Jewish Education Alliance's orchestra, in which Ed was a member, to entertain at the Levindale nursing home, along with serving ice cream and cake, all as a way to tie in a Bar Mitzvah celebration with an act of visiting the sick and elderly. Leonard's was the last Bar Mitzvah to be celebrated in the Lloyd Street synagogue before it closed.

The memory that lingers for the Attman boys is how their parents took interest and pride in them. Every Friday night, at the Sabbath table, after Harry made Kiddush, he had each of the boys make Kiddush. During the meal, Harry would ask them what they had learned that week in Hebrew school and, recalls Leonard, "how we are supposed to act in a traditional way." Following the *benching* (Grace After Meals), Harry and the children would sing *zemiros*, the songs associated with the Sabbath. Leonard still remembers fondly that on the walks to and from synagogue on Saturday morning, holding his father's hand, his father would question him about that week's Torah portion.

Ida was always the mother, advising them on ways to dress and act in public, helping them plan for their future, caring about their needs. One example stands out. After Ed was drafted into the army in 1941, the family worried about his safety. This concern increased when they did not receive any mail or hear from him for a month. One day, an individual came into the store and told Harry that he thought he saw Eddie on a newsreel being shown at a movie house on Lexington Street. It was a brief segment, he said, but it looked like Eddie was among a group of soldiers exercising on a ship somewhere in the Atlantic Ocean heading for North Africa. When she heard this, Ida immediately took a streetcar to see the newsreel.

"I went with her and recall it vividly," Leonard recounted in a taped interview for the Jewish Americans series. "Whatever the movie was wasn't important. We waited for the newsreel. And sure enough, when the newsreel came on, there were a group of guys standing on a ship, exercising in their shorts and shirts, and we saw my brother."

Ida was enthralled, alternately cheerful and tearful. She stayed and waited through the repeat of the movie until the newsreel came on again. And she then stayed to see the newsreel a third time.

"My mother stayed and saw the newsreel until midnight, until after the movies closed," said Leonard.

In coming days, Ida went back "day after day" until the newsreel showing Eddie was deleted from that part of the news.

By the end of World War II, Attman's Delicatessen was a well-known fixture on Lombard Street. As the oldest of the Attman boys, Ed, on his return from military service, was looking to start a career and a family. Harry and Ida could now turn their attention to helping Ed—and later, Seymour and Leonard—launch the next phase of their lives. The Attman brothers would have a special foundation on which to start. Their parents had already set a memorable example, showing each of them how to build a successful business while raising a family with lasting, meaningful values.

Chapter Four

"MUCH MORE THAN PAPER": EDWARD CREATES A MULTI-STATE ENTERPRISE

"Ed has such a positive attitude. He has a dogged determination and works very hard for his customers. He also has high integrity, a man of his word. When you combine those traits, you have the ingredients for success."

— Jim Alexy, CEO, Network Services Co., a $7 billion global distribution organization to which Acme Paper & Supply belongs as one of only 82 members in the U.S.

Since its opening in 1915, Attman's Delicatessen has offered the Attman family many benefits. The store provided an income for the parents and an opportunity for their children, as future entrepreneurs, to see how a business should operate and customers treated. For Ed, the Delicatessen afforded an additional and special benefit: It was where he met his future wife, who would become a life-long partner in his own business.

Mildred Cohen was sixteen when Ed, three years older, first noticed her. She had come to the store with her mother and father to shop.

"I was really impressed the first time I saw her," Ed recalls. "She was attractive and dressed very nicely. She caught my eye."

Her parents, Abraham and Rose Cohen, had recently moved to the area from the Essex section of Baltimore, where her father owned and operated the New Essex movie theater. A graduate of Kenwood High School, she would soon enroll in what is today the University of Baltimore to earn an A.A. degree in accounting. At the time, Ed was studying at the college for a degree in business administration. They met again at the school.

During this time, on February 7, 1942, four months before his class's graduation, Ed was drafted into the army. Since he had enough credits to graduate (as a day school student, he was allowed to take extra night classes at no additional charge and by doing so he had completed his course work in 3½ years), he was allowed to come back to Baltimore for the June graduation. He thereby became the first member of the Attman family to graduate college. At the graduation ceremony, he found that Mildred was also there, graduating with her A.A. degree. They struck up another conversation, and she invited him to a graduation party at her house.

To paraphrase the line made famous by the movie *Casablanca* that came out in that year, it was "the beginning of a beautiful relationship."

When he went back into the army, Ed and Mildred began corresponding and she would send him, he recalls fondly, "packages of goodies." This continued until, with the war winding down in Europe, Ed returned home from the service in June 1945. Interestingly, Ed would have been sent to the war still raging with Japan, as happened with many of his fellow soldiers, some of whom lost their lives, but he had never taken a furlough during the three years he was in the service and so earned enough points to be released at the end of May.

"When I got back, I called Mildred's house and her father answered. She wasn't there, so I said I would call back at six o'clock. I learned later he told her she better be there at six when I called," Ed says, with a chuckle.

Mildred's father, Abraham, who had served in the U.S. Army in World War I, had developed a liking for Ed, now a fellow veteran. He later brought Ed into the Jewish War Veterans. (A fascinating aspect about Mildred's father is that he was a war veteran because he had volunteered to go into the army in place of his brother, who had been drafted shortly after getting married, and he even used his brother's name throughout his military service. His act of brotherly love almost bordered on the ultimate sacrifice. Abraham Cohen wound up fighting in the intense Battle of Verdun in the Argonne Forest. In another reflection of his kindheartedness, he went into the lending business after the war, but during the Depression would not press for repayment from many of his stressed borrowers.)

Ed and Mildred started dating that June. They attended shows at the Lyric Theater, where her family had season tickets and Ed had tickets nearby. They also went to shows in New York City and to such Manhattan night spots as the Copacabana, the Latin Quarter, and the Cotton Club. They visited the city's Jewish area, dining at Ratner's dairy restaurant and then, joined by their parents, at the noted kosher restaurant, Lou G. Siegel. "Our parents enjoyed our mutual company," Ed recalls.

Ed and Mildred also spent time talking and learning about each other on the train trips up and back from New York. By the fall of that year, on the second night of the holiday of Succoth, Ed proposed, giving Mildred a ring. "It was a happy holiday," Ed remembers. "A joyous *yontif.*"

On March 3, 1946, they married. Mildred was 23, having been born August 17, 1923. Ed was 26. The wedding took place less than a year after he had returned from serving three years in the U.S. army during World War II.

Those three years were an important time in Ed's life, providing him with indelible memories. When he went into the army in 1942, the war was at its height. By mid-1942, the German army had swept across the face of Europe and into North Africa. The newsreel in which Ida saw Ed aboard a military ship was a rare glimpse into how the Allies were countering that threat. Ed was among 200,000 troops being transported on thousands of ships to North Africa to repel the advancing Axis forces and set the stage for pushing the Germans back into Europe.

"We were on the water for 30 days and nobody knew where we were going," he recalls. "We first went to England where forces were being gathered for the invasion of North Africa. Many of us were put on board the Queen Mary and then sent down to Algiers, one of the big drop-off points in North Africa, where we were moved to such places as the Arzew seaport in Oran."

During the voyage, Ed was stationed on guard duty near where mutton was stored for serving to the men, which was done three times a day. "The stench of that mutton still lingers in my mind. I can't have lamb 'til this day." Ed lived on lima beans during much of the trip.

The military enterprise in which Ed was a part was so massive that "whenever I looked out at the ocean all I could see were ships from many countries."

Upon arrival in the African continent, Ed, who had been trained in the use of radar, was assigned to radar units that over time were moved from Oran in northwest Algeria to Tunisia to Morocco. The army used these large radar installations, comprised of one-ton panels, to track enemy planes. Commanders deployed the units in all types of conditions, usually muddy, and their crews, who lived in tents, had to be constantly on alert. "Every day, something different was happening. We were always moving."

Eventually, Ed's unit was moved to Sardinia and then to Italy, where they landed in Naples. They then proceeded to Rome, eventually moving all the way up to Milan. When the war ended, Ed was stationed in Pisa.

All of this was a part of the Allied effort to defeat one of the Nazis' leading military strategists, Field Marshall Erwin Rommel, known as "the Desert Fox." When Ed and his fellow soldiers arrived in North Africa, Rommel's army had already been defeated in the major battle of El Alamein. But the new arrivals gave reinforcement to the Allied forces and, as Ed recounted, "put Rommel on the road. It broke up his force. He had to split up into different parts of North Africa to protect himself. It was also a tremendous surprise to the Germans, because everyone expected the counter-offensive to come first in Europe."

As a result, the Germans were prevented in North Africa from sweeping eastward to control the Suez Canal and to conquer Palestine, where they would have undoubtedly murdered the thousands of Jews living there and destroyed the physical reminders of the 3000-year Jewish presence in the Holy Land. Instead, the stage was set for the Allies to invade Italy, push into the underbelly of Nazi-held Europe, and win the war.

When the war in Europe ended in June, 1945, Ed returned home via a 10,000-mile trip by ship, transport, plane, and train that took him to South Africa, Brazil, and Florida. Coming back to the United States, he found a happy but weary populace. The war had been won, but with it had come years of deprivation, sacrifice and shortages on the home front. A host of products and materials were still in short supply. Ed remembers that leading executives were making $28 a week and working six days a week. Income from the deli was small. Before the war, a loaf of rye bread was 12 cents, and bagels and kaiser rolls were selling for 25 cents a dozen. After the war, prices rose, but still profits were meager. Attman's Delicatessen was selling corned beef for $1.85 a pound. Sandwiches were a quarter. Two cans of tuna sold for 25 cents and Maine sardines were selling for three cans for a dime.

At this time, Ed discovered a gratifying fact about the family situation. When he had gone into the service, he knew his father was heavily in debt from the Depression years and several unsuccessful business ventures with others, but upon his return Ed learned that his father had "little by little" paid off all his debts, an effort which greatly impressed Ed.

And so Ed, a veteran of the war, the first college graduate in his family, was faced with what to do with his life. After he and Mildred became engaged, they began planning their future for when they married. His mother had one strong piece of advice. Ida did not want him to go into the family business or into any similar line of work involving the preparation of food. She did not want to see him working the long hours like his father or having to deal with perishable food. Instead, she had another thought, based probably on her awareness of a non-food commodity always needed in delis.

"She recommended I go into paper, because paper never spoils," Ed remembers.

The idea was almost an eerie echo of the 'find a need and fill it' type of thinking that had guided Harry with his use of comb and scissors to earn money as a barber on his voyage to America, and was the basis of Napoleon Hill's popular *Think and Grow Rich* book.

Following Ida's advice, on April 1, 1946, just three weeks after their wedding, Ed and Mildred launched a company selling coarse paper products used for packaging purposes. At the suggestion of his brother Seymour, they looked for a name for their business that started with the letter 'A' so that it would be listed among the first names in the telephone directory. They eventually decided to call their enterprise Acme Paper & Supply Company.

To begin their business, Ed and Mildred rented a 1500 square foot garage at 21 South Front Street in East Baltimore from Scherlis & Katz, a fish company, for $75 a month. The place was not far from the Attman's Delicatessen on Lombard Street. At the beginning, Ed and Mildred had no money, no employees, no car or truck, and, because of the lingering effects and shortages of the war, only six products to sell. These were butcher paper, paper towels, toilet tissue, two kinds of paper bags, and wax paper (for use in deli and dairy stores).

"Merchandise was in short supply then, especially paper products such as paper towels and toilet tissues. There were just a few major producers and they controlled the market," Ed remembers. Plus, Ed and Mildred faced another problem: the government controlled the pricing on certain products, which meant that one could not charge above a set price for those items.

Whatever profits they generated in those first years "were very, very small."

"It was a big struggle. I even worked for my father on the weekends for $30 to help make ends meet."

But Ed remembers, too, that "because of our efforts, we were growing all the time, from Day One."

That growth enabled Acme Paper & Supply Company to reach its 64th anniversary in 2010, with Ed still at the helm and three of his sons and four grandsons actively involved on a daily basis, plus a fourth son a participant in company matters as well.

And that steady, at times spectacular, growth enabled Acme Paper & Supply to become today one of the nation's largest distributors of paper products, disposable goods, janitorial supplies, retail packaging, and restaurant equipment. The company now operates out of a warehouse/office complex in Savage, Maryland, and a major distribution center in Richmond, Virginia. It has 200 employees, six divisions including a creative arm developing its own products, a fleet of 40 vans, trucks and tractor-trailers, and customers ranging from major league stadiums to schools, from the U.S. Congress to convenience stores, from hospitals to hotels. It has serviced such major events as the U.S. Open Golf Tournament in New York, Chicago and San Diego; Baseball All-Star games; World Series games in Philadelphia and Baltimore; and the playoff games for all four major sports. Representing some of the biggest manufacturers and suppliers in the country, Acme now offers more than 15,000 products, so many and so varied that the company slogan is now "Acme...much more than paper."

How did Acme Paper emerge from that rented garage on 21 South Front Street into a powerhouse business operating on a local, regional, even national basis? What are Ed Attman's business philosophies? How has the Attman legacy influenced him, his company, his children and grandchildren?

To find out, I visit with Ed at his office in Acme's office/warehouse complex in Savage, Maryland, which is off U.S. 1 between Baltimore and Washington, D.C. His demeanor is gracious, he has a ready smile, and he looks vigorous. His office décor is warm and bright. Displayed here are various family pictures with Mildred and their children, along with photos of Ed and his brothers with Muhammad Ali and with former Secretary of State Henry Kissinger. On the walls are indications of his generosity: A Save-A-Heart plaque "for making possible continuance of its Life-Saving Cardiac Care Project." A Bais Yaakov School for Girls acknowledgement of a major donation by Ed, along with other Attmans, to the memory of Ida and Harry Attman "for their noble generosity to Jewish education." An Israel Freedom Award from Israel Bonds and membership in Israel's Prime Minister Club "for exceptional participation in the program for the economic development of Israel." Here, too, is a Jewish National Fund Golden Book Certificate presented by Phyllis and Leonard Attman on Ed's 70th birthday.

Ed's corner office is flanked to his left by his son Ronald's office after which is son David's office. To his right is son Steven's office. Nearby are offices of his grandsons. Throughout the rest of the floor and one floor above are offices for sales and marketing executives and an open bank of cubicles for secretaries, clerks, and other assistants. The atmosphere is calm, efficient and business-like. Outside the building, Acme trucks and those from suppliers and manufacturers either sit in one of the warehouse bays or stand in line, their drivers waiting to pick up or deliver shipments of goods. The recently expanded parking lot is full, with several cars parked on grassy areas along its rim.

In that interview, and in later interviews with Ed's sons, employees and others, a picture emerges of a hard-working, family-oriented, entrepreneurial savvy person who has fashioned a story of success over six decades.

Consider first the supportive ties of the Attman family. Ida's advice to her son to "go into paper" could be seen as a 20-year precursor to that famous line in the 1967 award-winning movie *The Graduate*, where actor Dustin Hoffman's young character was advised that his best future was "just one word: plastic." But with

Ed, the advice about paper was motivated by Ida's desire that the next generation of Attmans would do better than earning a living in one of the laborious narrow-profit small-store operations then doing business along Lombard Street. The advice was also prophetic, based on what Ida was observing daily and on what was happening in post-war America's burgeoning economy and increasingly mobile society. Oddly enough, Ed would soon see plastic joining paper as material for disposable goods, so in going into paper he was also going into plastic.

If Ida provided the idea for Ed and Mildred's business, Harry provided the business sense. Over the years, Ed was able to observe his father's work ethic, the considerate way he handled customers, the consistent daily effort he made to build the family business, the strategic buying and selling of goods with small profit margins. Now, Harry also provided help and guidance in other ways. Because Ed had no credit, his father took him to a bank and opened an account for him, telling him to establish a good credit history by borrowing a little and paying it back on time, "even if I didn't need it." His father taught him that, for those customers who could not pay for a large order, to offer to co-sign a note with them and then take the note to a bank for the cash. Then, if later there are collection problems, the customers would also be indebted to the bank. "People will pay the bank faster than they'll pay you," his father told him. Harry also initially helped Ed secure hard-to-get canned food and paper products to sell. And since many business people patronized Attman's Delicatessen, Harry was able to introduce Ed to them so that in time they proved to be willing customers of Ed's as his business began to grow.

And then, too, there was Mildred, his wife. As Ida was for Harry,

Mildred was a business helpmate for Ed. From the beginning, she was involved. For awhile, she was the only other person in the business. She would take phone orders from Ed after he had made a sales call and then would have the order ready when Ed returned. With her degree in accounting, she helped set up accounting procedures for the company. Many days, Mildred would come down to the office by streetcar or her father would drive her down. She was so involved that she worked while pregnant with their first child and came into the office the morning of the day when she later gave birth.

Eventually, three of their four sons and four grandchildren would join the company on a daily basis. A fourth son, Gary, is involved as well. Ronald (born August 26, 1947), David (November 19, 1950), and Steven (November 9, 1956) would each go to work at Acme after graduating college. Gary (June 2, 1954) fulfilled his desire to become an attorney and went on to partner with Ed's brother, Leonard, in building a healthcare business, but Ed made certain Gary was an equal partner with his brothers in Acme's operations. "We get together and discuss matters concerning Acme. As brothers, we have an open book about the business," says Gary.

Even while raising their children, Mildred would continue to help. After they moved to a home in northwest Baltimore, she would take the streetcar downtown to Acme Paper's office and then go back home to have dinner ready for the family.

Gary remembers how his father, to save money, would call the house and ring once, then hang up, a sign that he was on his way home. It was also a sign of his humble beginnings. Nonetheless, Ed was a good dresser who would occasionally treat himself with fine clothes and shoes. He and Mildred also made certain that their boys looked well-dressed and developed a sense of style.

Although Ed worked long days, he would still make time to show up for his sons' little league ball games, often coming around the fifth inning. And both parents would go to every PTA meeting and graduation, which was not always easy. When Gary secured, with the help of his Uncle Leonard, a coveted role as a congressional page in Washington, DC, and for two of his high school years worked for several members of Congress, he was schooled at the Capitol Page School in Washington and attended classes held at the Library of Congress. Gary's parents never missed a PTA meeting at Gary's school in Washington. Along with 49 other pages, Gary graduated high school in a ceremony that took place in the White House Rose Garden, where, with Ed and Mildred watching proudly, the Vice President of the United States presented Gary his diploma.

Ed also showed his children a sense of allegiance and devotion to religion. He prays daily. To honor the memory of Mildred's parents when they passed away, he went to the synagogue every day and evening to say the memorial prayer for them, just as he did for his own parents. He also does this on the anniversaries of the passing of other family members. He does not work on Saturday and does not open Acme on the Sabbath.

The seeds of Acme Paper & Supply Company's success can be seen in the shrewd way in which Ed went about starting and building what became a multi-state enterprise.

Consider how he dealt with the shortages of product in those first years after the war.

"People then were very appreciative of young people like me who were coming back from the war. They would say to me if I could get a product for the same price they were paying, they would buy from me. So I found out what they were paying and either tried to obtain it for less or sold it at the same price I paid so I could get other business from them. I even sometimes paid over the market price to secure supplies I could use to get into stores to sell other products," he says.

"The fish company that owned the building where I first started showed me what they were buying at what price, so I worked to get it for less. They became a good customer."

He found out that the market down south was not as strong as in Maryland. As a result, various southern companies could not sell all of the allotments they had. "So I found I could get products from there, and even paying for freight I could still sell products competitively up north."

Interestingly, Ron repeated this approach in the 1970s during a shortage of paper bags in the country. He kept calling around until he found that he could secure bags from a Boise-Cascade paper bag mill in Oregon. As a result, he was able to obtain an order for over $100,000 from the U.S. Army—at the time the largest order Acme had ever received.

Ed also traveled to Philadelphia where by means of an uncle, Jack Shapiro who was in the wholesale candy and tobacco business, he made contact with a supplier in the novelty business.

"People had money and were willing to buy good products. The problem was getting the product."

Adding to his problem of getting products was the fact that only a few major manufacturers existed in the coarse paper industry and they controlled the market. These manufacturers "wouldn't even look at me." To counter this, Ed went to companies "lower on the totem pole but would sell to me. They saw to it that we would be competitive."

He also learned to whom his competitors were selling and approached these potential customers. "Some bought from me and some didn't," but his list of customers was starting to grow. When visiting a customer, Ed always took with him some new item to let people know that his company was different.

Ed would begin his day by delivering whatever orders he had generated the day before. At midday, he would return to have lunch with Mildred (they would take the phone off the hook so they would appear busy if anyone called). In the afternoon, after 2 o'clock, he would go on another round of sales calls.

At the beginning, because he did not have a car, Ed would call on potential customers within walking distance of his office, walking farther and farther as he added more new territory. First, he would go to West Baltimore Street. Then to Market Place. Then to Pennsylvania Avenue.

"It was all by walking, little by little," he says.

He knew many of these nearby merchants, either from meeting them in the delicatessen or from his walks. And slowly he began adding customers. Other stores along Lombard Street, even competitors of his father's, bought from him: napkins, cups, toilet tissue.

"They needed service and I wasn't that far away," he says. He also learned that "if you treated people fairly, you would have the business."

Sussman and Lev, Vienna Restaurant, Holzman Bakery, Pastore's, Ginsburg Produce, Stone's Bakery, Coney Island Grill, Jack's Corned

Beef: These were some of his early customers from the Lombard Street area.

Then later, after he obtained a car, he went to west and south Baltimore, to the small merchants in the areas of Whitelock Street, Garrison Avenue and Park Heights: places where Jewish people were shopping.

As the post-war economy began picking up, opportunities for additional business began increasing. New stores were opening and existing stores were adding branches to service a population that was moving into newly constructed neighborhoods springing up farther from the center of the city. "The owners of these stores, satisfied with the way we were treating them, gave us more business."

To help with deliveries, he paid a person he knew as Elijah, who had an old Cadillac with a large trunk, to transport goods. After a few months, he hired a relative of his father-in-law—Mildred's cousin, Charles Cohen—to help with sales. He also periodically relied on gypsy drivers and vehicles for delivering orders. It was not until almost twenty years later, in 1968, that he hired another person to help with sales and delivery. Among his first hires was Carl Smelkinson, who retired from Acme in 2006, and Leon Yoffee.

During this time, as he began handling more merchandise, Ed moved from renting a garage to renting a location on the corner of High and Low Streets, currently the site of the city's main U.S. post office, where he had twice the square footage at not much more rent. This move was followed, in 1961, by Ed's first purchase of a building. He bought at auction an 18,000 square foot facility at 1516 Register Street. Here, he had more space for storage, a garage with doors for easier pickup and delivery of goods, and a location in a neighborhood where more laborers were available. Acme Paper was located here for nine years until Ed was faced with another decision to keep expanding. The next move, in 1969, was to locate to a larger building at Sharp and Barre Streets in the Inner Harbor area.

At this time, Ed and Mildred's children started becoming more involved. As youngsters, they had expressed interest in being part of the company. In high school, during the summers when school was out, Ron along with David and Steven would drive down to Acme in Ron's Mustang, a drive in Baltimore's hot, humid daytime the boys still remember because the Mustang had no air conditioning They first began by working in the warehouse. "We learned how to make a pallet and how to pack the trucks," recalls Steven. From that beginning and in coming years, they gained experience in other areas of the company.

The result, says David, is that "we all grew up in the business."

Ronald, as the oldest, made a career decision and life-long commitment to the business when he turned 21 and was graduating from University of Maryland. Ed asked him if he was interested in working full-time at Acme. Ron replied, "Yes, no doubt about it."

Ed's invitation and Ron's acceptance has become a hallmark of the Attmans: a closeness of family as one generation works with and helps the other. David and Steven, after they each graduated from the University of Maryland, soon followed Ron into Acme Paper. Although Gary had assisted periodically at Acme, his desire was always to be an attorney. After he also graduated from the University of Maryland, he earned a law degree, clerked for a federal judge, and then went to work at Gordon Feinblatt, a major Baltimore law firm. He eventually joined with his Uncle Leonard to form a healthcare company, which became FutureCare.

"We worked as a family. We paid the boys according to their needs. I gave to them before I took mine," Ed recalls.

But Acme was growing and expanding, with new products to sell, new clients to service, new plans to be implemented. Soon Ronald, David, and Steven married and began raising families of their own. Acme's growth was providing incomes for not only Ed and Mildred and three of their children's families, but also for more than 200 sales people, support staff, and drivers (or, as Steven notes, his father would say that Acme employs "over 200 families").

And now another Attman generation has joined the company. Four of Ed and Mildred's grandchildren—Ron's sons Scott, Andy and Keith and Steven's son Michael—all went to work full-time at Acme after graduating college. Scott and Andy are involved in account development and Keith serves as manager of purchasing. Michael, the most recent to join, is being groomed to go into sales. As Ron told his sons when they came into Acme Paper, "I expect you to work. I didn't bring you in so I could take a salary cut."

Today, Acme's primary corporate offices and warehouse are located in Savage, Maryland, near Jessup, a location chosen for being between the company's major markets of Baltimore and Washington and central to its reach throughout the Mid-Atlantic region. The complex was built in 1979, expanded in 1985 and again in 2001, features a warehouse with a capacity of 3.5 million cubic feet, a 20,000 square feet headquarters, and 19 truck bays: a far cry from Acme's beginnings using a rented garage for storage and a used car with a large trunk to make deliveries.

Over the years, Acme grew not only by increasing business among current clients and constantly seeking new clients, but also by diversifying and acquiring other companies.

"I believed in diversification," says Ed. "Early in our history, I did business with a neighbor who was in the rag business. When we eventually bought his business, this was our first taste of the janitorial business. We then bought Baer Supply, which got us into janitorial equipment."

Ed took Acme into the industrial packaging business by purchasing National Paper Company, and then followed this with the acquisition of the Professional Paper Company, another industrial packaging-type enterprise.

In 1991, to solidify its presence in Virginia, Acme purchased the Hamilton Paper Company in Richmond. In 2005, to add further to its industrial packaging division and to meet its increasing business in Virginia and North Carolina, Acme purchased the Richmond division of Kent H. Landsberg Company. Soon after, Acme expanded here too, operating today in Richmond out of a 90,000 square foot distribution center.

The purchase of KayBoys in 1999 strengthened Acme's position in retail packaging. In 2002, Acme established a restaurant equipment and supply division to be able to offer a customer starting a restaurant the needed equipment and supplies, from the planning stage until the facility opens and is operating.

"Being diversified is very important," Ed emphasizes. "For instance, a person opens a restaurant; you get his equipment business. Then you can sell him other things for a restaurant."

Acme's strategy of diversification has enabled it to capitalize on the ever-continuing development of new products and the rising consumer demand for those products that has marked the U.S. marketplace since the Second World War.

"When I started, there were no plastic bags, cups or cutlery. There was no decent packaging. In paper products, there were no two-ply toilet tissues, no three-ply napkins. Even shopping bags have changed. We would have to staple handles to the bags by hand. Today the market is unlimited and we can get the best of products in paper, plastics, janitorial supplies and equipment," Ed says.

Acme has also established a division, Alpha Products, specializes in producing customized packaging, including promotional items, to provide creative solutions for Acme's customers, especially in the sports and entertainment industries. The division is headed by Jim Haire, former regional sales manager of Sweetheart/Maryland Cup Company, who is now a 25-year veteran of Acme Paper and serves as director of sales and marketing.

One of Alpha's unique food service packaging items is the Alpha Concession Tray, the largest food-carrying tray now in use in stadiums and arenas. Previously, operators of concession stands provided patrons with only small cardboard trays in which to carry food items. The Alpha tray, made out of sturdy heavier gauge paper board, has a design that enables customers to carry back to their seats up to four drinks of any size, plus such items as nachos, peanuts, and hot dogs. Invented and co-designed by Jim Haire and Steve Attman, this tray is now considered a significant development in boosting concession sales wherever it is offered. As an indication of the tray's uniqueness, Acme received a patent for its design.

Acme also received a patent for the Alpha Division's introduction of 'The Kid's Home Plate Meal.' This five-sided carton in the shape of a baseball home plate offers a creative way for a sporting event concessionaire to appeal to children by presenting the elements of a full meal in a unique container with a baseball theme.

"In our industry, there are many common products in disposable single-service items available from many distribution sources. What sets Acme apart is our ability to introduce shapes, sizes and configurations that are marketable," says Jim Haire. "That's why we try to create a need for more innovative products with some special design characteristic."

One such item was a Glow-in-the-Dark souvenir beverage cup that Acme introduced for a chain of movie theaters to use in an anti-drug campaign they were promoting. The cup, along with an anti-drug message printed on its outside, would glow when a patron carried it into the darkness of the theater.

Alpha has designed many souvenir and promotional cups to satisfy both the fan's thirst and the desire for a collectible game souvenir. It was Alpha that produced a special four-color 32 ounce souvenir cup to commemorate Cal Ripken's retirement from baseball. Commemorative cups have also been created for baseball's league championship series, the Olympic Games held in Atlanta, and the 1994 Woodstock Festival.

To what does Jim attribute Acme's success?

"Our retention of clients is extremely high in an industry prone to change, and I think it's a tribute to Acme's service and sales representation. Our customer satisfaction is very high. It's based on our purchasing the right product at the right price and getting the order to the client at the right time. Our order fill-rate—the percentage of time that an order is delivered correctly and on schedule—is close to 100 percent." One way in which this is accomplished is that Acme was early in installing GPS systems on its trucks and continually monitoring each delivery with a computer system that tracks the hundreds of orders a day that each driver is making. In addition, Acme's warehouse is totally computerized, enabling the company to locate any of its 15,000 products at any time.

Jim also cites Acme's "history of hiring and retaining good people." He pointed to the fact the company has three regional sales managers and 30 experienced sales people, all of which are supported by divisional personnel. "It's having the people in the field maintaining and growing existing customers while pursuing new opportunities."

But coupled with that is Ed's treatment of his employees.

"The most important aspect of Eddie is his ability to treat all people as equal," says Jim. "I've seen this many times: from presidents of corporations to the lowliest man on the street. It is an incredible quality, especially from a work viewpoint. He treats the newest, most elementary employee with the same respect and appreciation as he does his family. He's almost like Will Rogers. Ed Attman never met a person he didn't respect."

Jim notes another quality that has resulted in high staff morale. "He's generous. He's not all about what success means, financially or materialistically. To him, his success is to see everyone else succeed. He's not the kind to take the last piece of bread. I see that quality in his sons. They're respectful of all employees."

Products. Service. Creativity. Selling skills. Creating a connection with clients at various levels in an organization. Jim mentioned each of these elements as reasons for Acme's growth and success. "Get a little foothold with a client, offer good service, and eventually business expands," he says, and it sounds very much like what Ed Attman learned from his father and in his early days building Acme.

"A significant amount of major business is developed and maintained on relationships," Jim states. "We are really not a price seller. If you sell on price, you're out on price."

"My father is very visionary," says Steven, who cites Ed's willingness to make such major decisions, and investments, as building the warehouse/office complex in Savage, Maryland (which, according to Ron, doubled business). David points out that Ed was "on top of new products. He would never say no to getting something different or trying new things," whether it was innovative products, technology, or ways of selling. Among other examples his sons cited: Ed was an early supporter of a company web site, was one of the first to use voice mail in the office and to put GPS in trucks, was among the first to sell such products as clear plastic cups and plastic straws instead of paper straws, even led the way in convincing Acme's hospital clients to use Styrofoam and plastic instead of china for patient meals.

And now, in response to the growing need for environmentally friendly products, Acme has developed a full-line of 'green' products and eco-friendly alternatives. As stated on its website, "Acme Paper believes that environmental consciousness is a shared responsibility." In that regard, Acme offers a complimentary Green Products Analysis to current and potential customers "to learn what products you're using now and the green alternatives best suited for your operations." With each of its six divisions able to offer such alternatives, Acme has assisted in the implementation of green products with outdoor entertainment operations, sports complexes, school systems and hotels. Acme has even helped Congress "Go Green."

Scott Attman was an early advocate of green products. Utilizing the same innovative spirit that his grandfather had embraced in bringing new products to Acme's customers in the 1950s, Scott foresaw how green products would become an important factor in the region and in government. In 2008, Restaurant Associates of New York retained Acme to partner in supplying the six restaurants and cafeterias of the U.S. House of Representatives with environmentally friendly food service items. This was part of Speaker Nancy Pelosi's "Greening the Capitol" plan to make the House more environmentally friendly, and Scott took the initiative in working with the House of Representative's Green program. He sourced all the products that were needed to give the House a program with 100 percent compostable products, which even included bottled water that was packaged in compostable bottles. This, in fact, became the only bottled water that was permitted to be sold in the House food service operations. Acme now also supplies green products to the cafeterias at the U.S. State Department, the Pentagon, and the Department of Energy.

As the business grew, Ed assigned Ron, David and Steven each to a different, though complementary, function.

Ron oversees the day-to-day operations, serving virtually as the company's general manager, involved in the range of major and minor decisions that confront an ever-growing American business today. In this capacity and with more than 40 years experience, he has also risen in the industry. After being active on its board, he was elected in 2001 to serve a two-year term as chairman of the board of Network Services Company, the largest distribution organization in North

America, comprising companies involved in providing the full range of paper, plastic and janitorial supplies. Network now has members in 32 countries, with 82 members and 306 distribution centers in the United States. It is a unique operation in that its member companies, which have to be accepted into membership after a rigorous review of product expertise, reputation, ethics and profitability, own the organization. Membership provides Acme, a member since 1990, with greater buying power with large suppliers and manufacturers from around the world, which enables Acme to pass these cost savings onto its customers. Network also enables Acme and fellow members, with their access to Network's distribution centers throughout the country, to sell and service national accounts. After serving as Chairman, Ron remains active on three Network committees.

David's role is to maintain relations with manufacturers and suppliers. Ed has always acknowledged that one of the reasons for Acme's success has been its good relationship with its suppliers. The irony here is that when he started his business Ed could not persuade the major manufacturers to do business with him. Interestingly, as Ed has noted, not one of those manufacturers is in business today. They have all sold out to others. To maintain good relations with the 25 to 30 key manufacturers today, as well as other suppliers, David meets regularly with their top executives. His objective is to make certain that Acme has access to the latest products and best pricing available, and he works to resolve any issues.

Steven is responsible for new business development and the maintenance of relationships with major accounts, especially in healthcare, such as hospitals and nursing homes, and in the food service industry. He works closely with Jim Haire on soliciting new accounts, some of which could take years of pursuit before clinching. He worked for several years on landing the concession account that services the Baltimore Orioles, actually beginning the attempt the summer after he started full-time at Acme. Acme has now held the account since 1978, working over that time with three different concessionaires, first at Memorial Stadium and now at Oriole Park at Camden Yards. Jim says of Steven that he is "the sales ambassador for the company, carrying the Attman name throughout the area." In quoting his father's advice to 'set your sights high,' Steven says, "The lesson I have learned is 'Give me some meetings so that I can get in the door to show our concepts, then I know Acme can produce and we will have the account.'"

That energy, that willingness to work hard is what reverberates throughout the Attman family. It started with Harry. It can be seen with Ed, with his sons, and with his brothers. Steve has talked of the "incredible energy level" in his father and his uncles, Seymour and Leonard. David points out that it was 17 years before his father went on vacation. At the age of 90, Ed goes to the gym several times a week and works with a trainer.

Jim Haire, as head of the sales force, tells how Ed, in welcoming new sales people, always includes a comment that contains the essence of Attman business philosophy along with a touch of humor:

"You come to work for Acme, you can make a lot of money," Ed Attman will say to the new hire. "You only have to work a half day: 12 hours."

Ed may be joshing about such a standard, but it is a standard that he has seemingly always lived by. Gary remarks that his father is "very demanding on himself."

"He is a realist, he knows the reality of a situation, but he sets goals and is very persistent in pursuing them," Gary says.

Gary notes another aspect of his father that has contributed to his success. "He is the most decent, honest person. Honesty is part of his basic character. He does not do anything that is not consistent with those beliefs with which he was brought up. And he has conveyed these beliefs to us, his children."

Jim Alexy, who retired as CEO of Network Services Company, has had business and personal dealings with Ed and has observed him from various perspectives: as a supplier, when Jim was President of Sweetheart Cup in the 1980s and Acme was a customer, and now at Network, in which capacity he works to help Acme service its accounts. He has played golf with Ed and Ron and has been invited to Ed and Mildred's 50th wedding anniversary. "When I was at Sweetheart, if he was trying to get a piece of business in his area, he would constantly call and try to get the best deal for his customers. At Network, while I was CEO, he would also constantly call to represent his company for their growth."

What has also impressed Alexy, who has known Ed since 1983, has been the Attman family. "It's been my pleasure to know and do business with the Attmans. This is a wonderful family. I saw how close they are when they all showed up for Ed and Mildred's 50th wedding anniversary. It makes you feel good to see that, especially when things family-wise are falling apart elsewhere in our society."

That sense of family may be finding its highest expression in recent years in Ed's dedication to his wife, now in declining health with Alzheimer's. Ed has shown his constant devotion to Mildred in many ways. One such way: He takes her out to dinner every night, accompanied on a rotating basis by each son and spouse who gladly volunteered to be with them for the evening.

Says Ron, "The way my father takes care of my mother is really an inspiration to all of us. And we can see it's reciprocal. Even in her limited capacity, the way Mom looks at him, we know she cares for him and appreciates what he does for her."

"My father's love and devotion to my mother may be the greatest love story you'll ever see," Gary says. "This may be his ultimate legacy: his ability to return love and devotion to my mother who has given him so much."

On May 5, 2008, sixty-six years after Ed Attman graduated from the University of Baltimore, its Merrick School of Business honored him as the 2008 University of Baltimore Distinguished Entrepreneur. In presenting the award, Jim Kucher, Executive Director of the Entrepreneur Program, said, "Mr. Attman's business vision is a powerful inspiration for the emerging entrepreneurs we are training today." Anyone starting or growing a business could learn from Ed Attman's "funding and management of Acme Paper," which was termed "a showcase for all manner of business entrepreneurs."

The following year, in 2009, Ed presented a substantial gift to his alma mater "for the support, training and mentoring of students, alumni and others interested in developing small business start-ups." This new part of the university's Entrepreneurial Opportunity Center was named the Edward Attman and Mildred Cohen Attman Enterprise Hatchery. The Dean of U of B's business school, Darlene Smith, praised Ed as one of the school's leading alumni and said that his support "reveals the depth of his entrepreneurial mindset."

When he was honored with the University of Baltimore's

Entrepreneur Award, Ed told the audience what he had learned about how to succeed in the business world. "It means treating the customer as you would want to be treated, all the time. You are your customer's keeper. To me, the secret to success in business is no secret. It's work harder for the customer than you work for yourself, and price your product or service fairly. People like to do business with people they like…and trust."

As for specifics about Acme's enduring example of achievement, Ed stated, in an interview published in the Acme Paper newsletter on the occasion of the company's 60th anniversary, that he attributed Acme's success to the "good, dedicated people working for us" and that "our suppliers have been very cooperative and are a very important part of our growth."

He concluded by noting that three generations of the family were now working in the business: "In looking back, I would say that I have been very fortunate to have a wife, like Mildred, and children who don't look to just take out of the business; they contribute to it. That's my good fortune."

Chapter Five
"WORK IS A JOY": SEYMOUR CAPTIVATES CORNED BEEF ROW

*"Seymour was one of the greatest, gentlest,
nicest persons I ever met in my life."*

— State Senator Nathaniel J. McFadden,
Majority Leader of the Maryland Senate
Chair of the Baltimore City Senate Delegation
Senate President Pro Tem

On Thursday, August 20, 2003, Baltimore City put Seymour Attman on its map. In a ceremony hosted by Baltimore's mayor, a newly constructed street that linked Lombard and Pratt Streets, just a half block from Attman's Delicatessen and part of a renewal program for the neighborhood, was officially named 'Seymour Attman's Way.' The next day, the *Baltimore Sun* reported on the event in a four-column article with pictures, announcing that "Seymour Attman was such a fixture at his Lombard Street Deli that city officials have named a street after him." Mayor (and later Governor) Martin O'Malley along with Seymour's children Marc, Eileen, and Deborah were shown putting up a new street sign with Seymour's name on it. Also attending the ceremony were Congressman (later U.S. Senator) Benjamin Cardin and a crowd of elected officials, Attman family members, friends and the public.

Interestingly, the *Sun* noted that naming a street in honor of a person broke Mayor O'Malley's then current moratorium against such a practice. But Mayor O'Malley in his remarks said that in Seymour's case he was making an exception ("What good is mayoral prerogative if you can't suspend a moratorium?" he quipped). But the paper also cited wide support for the action and reported the sentiment that putting 'Seymour Attman's Way' on the city maps "was just the right way to honor a Russian Jewish immigrant's son who cared about the neighborhood's past and future."

Dedicating a road in the Lombard Street area to an Attman would have been well-deserved at any time, but the timing that day was sadly appropriate. Just about a year before on June 30, 2002, three weeks after suffering a heart attack, Seymour had passed away at the age of 76. Fittingly, he was working in the store when he collapsed.

Of all of Harry and Ida Attman's progeny, Seymour became the most involved with Attman's Delicatessen over the years. He was the one who, from the age of 16, worked on a daily basis with his father and took over management of the delicatessen when Harry died in 1968. It was he who led the business through the riots of the late 1960s, through the population shifts in the neighborhoods around the store, through the economic changes that needed to be made to keep the delicatessen flourishing. And fittingly, it is his son Marc who, although a successful optometrist and owner of a string of optical stores, took over after Seymour died and has helped firmly establish Attman's Delicatessen as an icon of Corned Beef Row and Jewish Baltimore. Together, Seymour and Marc worked to meet the considerable challenge of ensuring that a nearly 100-year-old business not only survives, but thrives.

Seymour's death, as his life, touched many people. The *Baltimore Sun* and the *Baltimore Jewish Times* published extensive obituaries and follow-up columns about him when he passed away. The *Sun* noted how Seymour "helped make the name Attman synonymous with Baltimore corned beef" and, in a caption beneath a photo taken of him in the doorway of the store a year before his death, reported that "Seymour Attman's deli regularly appears on lists of the top places to eat and visit in Baltimore." The *Jewish Times*, in an editorial entitled "Attman's Legacy," termed him "the last remnant, the ultimate survivor" of the era of early 20th century when the Lombard Street area neighborhood was the center of Jewish Baltimore: "In so many ways, Seymour Attman *was* Jewish Baltimore. It was in his veins, his brains, his mouth, his hands, and most of all, it was in his heart." An overflow crowd gathered at the Sol Levinson and Brothers funeral home for the ceremony at which Beth Tfiloh's Rabbi Mitchell Wohlberg and Chizuk Amuno's Rabbi Joel Zaiman spoke. Marc wrote a eulogy that Rabbi Zaiman read to the audience.

What caused this outpouring of feeling and sentiment?

Each speaker in his own way talked about an aspect of Seymour Attman that together painted a picture of an unusual individual. Rabbi Wohlberg related that every time he would see him, Seymour, instead of shaking his hand, would kiss him. He termed Seymour, who was generous and giving and full of life as "a classic, a real one-of-a-kind." Rabbi Zaiman talked of how Seymour, with his gregarious nature, his concern for others, was "a presence," "a character," in many ways "bigger than life." Marc's eulogy concluded with a call to think of his father in the way he would probably want: "When you remember Seymour Attman, remember his sandwiches, good heart, and the smile on his face whenever he saw you."

Seymour had a ready smile and generated smiles in others, but as with other hardy individuals who encounter and are able to triumph over adversity, those smiles were genuine for being hard-earned. For Seymour's life was difficult from the beginning. He was born at home on April 27, 1926, the second of three sons of Harry and Ida Attman. His older brother, Ed, then seven years old, who did not know his mother was pregnant, came home from school to find to his surprise that he now had a baby brother. Seymour's birth held another surprise. He was born without a right ear, a rare birth defect.

In a September 15, 1982, interview taped by Helen Sollins of the Jewish Historical Society of Maryland, Seymour talked about how his parents reacted to his handicap, especially his mother:

"I'm very happy for having the parents I had. And my mother went through hardship with me because I was born with one ear. She couldn't make it to the hospital with me and it took a lot out of her when I was born this way. And she really felt sorry for me. I used to have hair like a pageboy [to cover the area] when I went to school, so the boys thought that I was a girl. In those days, it wasn't such a stylish thing. I wanted to hide the ear, so I had a pageboy. I didn't get my hair cut [in a boyish style] almost until I was bar mitzvah. So I went through a little bit of a hassle as a kid."

Seymour could hear out of his left ear, but his parents, at considerable expense, took him to Dr. Page Davis, a pioneer in plastic surgery at Union Memorial Hospital who treated people from around the country. He fashioned a semblance of a right ear for Seymour, and Seymour remembers how the doctor never pressured for payment but his father would pay the doctor five or ten dollars at a time.

"My father respected him for taking care of me," Seymour recalled. "But like I said, it took a lot out of my mother when I was born this way. She was good to me."

In spite of what some would consider a disability that could have affected his relationships with others, causing him to be withdrawn, Seymour was outgoing and led an exuberant life that garnered many close friendships over the years. His nephew Gary believes Seymour's positive attitude about his disability may have enabled him to approach life in an unconventional, innovative way, resulting in his being able to build on his father's efforts to achieve even greater success with the store. Nothing seemed to deter Seymour, even in his early life when he could have been most vulnerable. In fact, Seymour always expressed fond memories of growing up.

Another factor about Seymour's success with operating the delicatessen was his appreciation for food and good cooking, something that came early to him in the Attman household. He talked especially about his mother's cooking. "I really enjoyed being in the kitchen and getting the smells and getting all the nostalgia," he said in that interview.

He talked of remembering "all the good things" his mother cooked and baked: the *kichellah*, Purim hamentashin with honey and poppy seeds made into little squares "like candies," blintzes, knishes, challah: all homemade. "Those days it wasn't as it is today. Everything is from the freezer or everything is commercially made. Anybody who is brought up food-wise like I am … can remember their parents as being real *ballabustas*."

He related how his mother would work all hours to accomplish the cooking and housework. "She did a lot of things late at night. Many times I would come in from playing, I would see like the dough which is kneaded, because she was making challah or something like that, and I would see it with a kitchen towel of some sort covered over the dough to make it rise or to keep it from rising. I used to watch my mother bake a lot of things." He pointed out that both of his sisters-in-law have some of his mother's recipes.

That nostalgia became one of the driving forces in Seymour's life. As he mentioned in the interview, "I have great joy and pleasures coming into my place today because it gives me a piece of my father's heritage."

Seymour's childhood and teenage years were a mixture of work and play.

Asked by the interviewer if he had much idle time as a child, he responded: "No, I worked a lot, but I played, but I didn't have the social life I really wanted."

He did recount how he would go to the Jewish Educational Alliance (the JEA), a popular social gathering place for the young located on Baltimore Street, to play basketball. He also went to Patterson Park where he roller-skated and played softball. Unlike his brothers who did not want to go, he went away to Camp Airy and enjoyed the experience. On Saturday afternoons after Sabbath services, he and friends would play Monopoly "for hours and hours and hours." They also "used to love to take long walks" on the Sabbath, walking as far as City College. He proudly pointed out how he was Shomer Shabbos then and would put his house key on a handkerchief he wrapped around his wrist so he would not be carrying on the Sabbath. He had decided, at the time, "to be very religious and adhere to Orthodox policies." He spoke proudly of how he enjoyed going to his family's *shul*, Shomre Shamares (today called the Lloyd Street Synagogue).

By his own admission, Seymour "wasn't too good a student." He received his Bar Mitzvah training from a private teacher who "taught me with patience." He had started his Jewish education at Yeshivah Chofetz Chaim (today, Talmudical of Baltimore), but his parents soon transferred him to Public School 93 on Central Avenue. "Sometimes I had a conflict of interest with the teachers," he said and his parents felt a change in his school setting would help him. After his Bar Mitzvah, Seymour went back to the Hebrew school. Later in life, after his mother passed away and Seymour began going to shul on a more daily basis, he spoke of how he "really did enjoy learning.

That's when I really got a kick out of history."

All in all, as he told the interviewer, he felt he had a happy childhood, but his one regret was that he did not do as much as he wanted because he worked a lot. But Seymour also enjoyed working, something he did full-time in the store from the age of 16. Here, in the family's business, he ultimately realized his potential, especially when he took full control after his father passed away in 1968. If the mantra of business success is to find a need and fill it, one might say that in one's personal life, the goal should be to find one's niche and fill it. For Seymour Attman, his niche was Attman's Delicatessen.

And he filled it with his own characteristic verve, humor, good nature, sense of marketing, and customer relations, all combined with knowledge of the delicatessen business he had learned by observing his father steer the store through decades of struggle into success.

According to his brother Ed, the store gained its greatest popularity when Seymour took over the day-to-day operations and largely phased out the grocery part of the business to concentrate on the delicatessen and introduced a wide variety of sandwiches and platters. Seymour regularly worked long hours, but always with a smile and a ready laugh at a joke. Labeling sandwiches with funny names—from 'Tongue Fu' to 'Our Wurst Sandwich'—was pure Seymour. Buying the building next door and tearing down the adjoining wall to create a sit-down area, and labeling it the Kibbitz Room, was Seymour's idea. He also expanded into providing a catering business and hosting private parties. At one time, he even opened Attman's Delicatessens in five locations around the city and suburbs, but soon realized that delicatessens needed on-site owner management to succeed.

Seymour also carried on his father's tradition of being close to his customers and good to his help. "I still remember how nice Seymour and his father were to me when I was a little girl growing up in Little Italy and my mother took me and my brother to Lombard Street and to Attman's," recalls Giovanna Aquia-Blattermann, who still lives in Little Italy and today owns Gia's, an upscale beauty salon in Mt. Washington. "The Attmans introduced us to pickled onions and corned beef, giving us free chips of corned beef on wax paper when we came into the store." The hard chips of corned beef remain her favorite part of corned beef to this day, she told me.

She especially remembers how Seymour "always had a smile on his face" and joked around with Gia and her brother. "He was very gregarious."

Seymour was well-liked by the Italians who lived nearby in Little Italy. At one point, he went to Public School No. 2, which had many Italian students, and Gia recalls how Seymour would socialize with them, even attending their dances.

"Whenever he walked through our area, he would be greeted with 'How you doing, Seymour?' He literally owned the streets of Little Italy."

As a result of her growing up so close to the Jewish community around Lombard Street and her family shopping at the street's variety of Jewish-owned stores ("that was our mall"), Gia says that "it took me a long time to realize Jews weren't Italians."

Seymour and his father also befriended many African-Americans in the neighborhood. One was Nathaniel McFadden, who grew up in the Flag House Courts public housing project, a 1960s inner city rehabilitation program of high-rise apartment buildings in the Lombard Street area until being demolished in 2000 for redevelopment with mixed-use housing. McFadden first worked on Lombard Street when at the age of 12 he was hired to clean out the stalls in the stores selling live chickens. Seymour, recognizing Nathaniel's potential, counseled him on staying in school and embarking on a career. McFadden eventually earned bachelor and master's degrees, won election to the Baltimore City Council, and then was elected to the Maryland Senate, rising to a position of power in the State House as Majority Leader of the Senate, President Pro Tem of the Senate, Chair of the Baltimore City Senate Delegation, and a leader of the black caucus in the legislature.

"He was one of the greatest, gentlest, nicest persons I ever met in my life," Senator McFadden was quoted in *The Sun* report on the street-naming ceremony for Seymour. "When so many businesses left, Mr. Seymour Attman had a commitment to this city." The article reported that McFadden was one of those instrumental in persuading the mayor to name the street in Seymour's honor.

That good relationship with the area's black community led to a remarkable result when Baltimore City suffered through the 1968 rioting in the aftermath of the assassination of Martin Luther King, Jr. During three days in April of that year, looting erupted and more than 900 fires were set in Baltimore. While rioters ravaged the inner city and either broke into or set fire to many stores, especially along Lombard Street, Attman's Delicatessen was largely spared. In fact, although snipers often kept the fire department from entering an area to put out fires, when Smelkinson's Dairy Store next to Attman's was totally engulfed in flames, the neighborhood allowed fire fighters in to keep fires from spreading to the delicatessen.

In its coverage of the riots in the Lombard Street area, The Sun reported on this phenomenon and quoted Seymour after he was able to return to inspect the store:

"It's hard to believe. They broke the windows, but they didn't loot. Not a nickel of stock is missing. The police and firemen did a wonderful job. Look at next door; completely gone. And all we got was some water damage. It's a miracle."

The riots so affected Seymour's daughter, Debbie, 11 years old at the time, that she clipped out numerous newspaper articles covering the riot and mounted them, along with her handwritten comments, in a 14-page scrapbook she entitled, "Destruction of Baltimore." She started the scrapbook with a black and white photo taken by a family member of Seymour standing in front of the delicatessen after the riots. She ended her compilation with a declaration: "I am glad that my father's store was not badly hurt. I hope everything will stop and get back to the <u>best, best, best</u> city."

Seymour was not all work. He liked to visit restaurants, both to enjoy dining out and to privately critique and learn from others in the food business. He was a fan of boxing, dressed in fashionable clothes, and kept up-to-date on the latest cars. His ready wit led him to enjoy and tell jokes, even at his own expense. Once after buying a new auto, he quipped, in a reference to his having only one ear, that he understood the car had a very good stereo system. He also found time to date, marry, raise a family, go through a divorce, and remarry. But he also experienced the death of his ex-wife as well as his second wife and, in an especially wrenching tragedy, suffered the loss of a son.

On February 23, 1950, Seymour married Ruth Vatapsky, 23, the oldest of three daughters of Samuel and Tobey Vatapsky

(Ruth's sisters were Sally and Norma). Seymour and Ruth had four children: Marc (born October 11, 1951), Eileen (November 27, 1952), Deborah (May 11, 1957), and Stuart (February 29, 1960). Interestingly, each was born on a special day: Marc on Yom Kippur, Eileen on Thanksgiving, Deborah on Mother's Day, and Stuart on a Leap Year day. The children remember Ruth "as a strong force in the family and a very loving Jewish mother." She worked with Seymour in the store, especially on weekends. Eileen and Deborah remember how on Saturday nights, after closing the store, their parents would bring home servings of turkey, corned beef, and brisket, along with fresh hot rolls from Stone's Bakery on Lombard Street, and make a one a.m. deli party for their children and their friends. "It was great," Eileen says.

Ruth was also known for the care she gave as a daughter-in-law to Seymour's father, Harry, and to her sister, Sally. After Seymour's mother passed away, Seymour, who had moved into a house on Northbrook Road in Pikesville, next door to Ed and down the block from Leonard, converted the garage into an apartment for his father. Ruth kept the apartment clean for him and cooked for him, and every Friday night Harry had Sabbath dinner with them. Ruth's sister, Sally, was born with a brittle bone genetic disorder, called osteogenesis imperfecta, which made her an invalid. The doctors told Ruth's parents that Sally would not live past 13, but instead of placing her in an institution, her parents decided to care for her at home and Ruth played a key part in her daily care. Sally eventually lived to the age of 65.

After 27 years of marriage, Seymour and Ruth divorced. The children considered the divorce "tragic" and ascribed it to their father possibly passing through a mid-life crisis. According to Eileen, her mother never really recovered from the divorce. But Ruth stayed very much involved with the Attman family. According to Marc, Ruth was loved not only by her children, but "by her nieces and nephews as though she was their mother, even after the divorce, and she felt the same." Born December 8, 1926, she died October 22, 1988. But before her death, says Eileen, Ruth and Seymour "had their peace."

In 1981, Seymour married Elinor Dopkin, who passed away in 2000. From his children, Seymour knew the joy of three grandchildren—Alison, Jessica, and Chelsea—plus a great-grandchild, Samuel. From his second marriage, he had an extended family of Melinda, Lisa, and Kimberly.

On Monday, November 14, 1994, Seymour received a shocking phone call that altered and seriously dampened the last eight years of his life. He was informed that Stuart, the son who had been working with him full-time for 20 years since the age of 14, who loved the delicatessen business and intended to make it his career, who had made a success as head of the catering arm of Attman's, had died that morning while on a one-week vacation in Negril, Jamaica. He had been standing on a cliff overlooking the ocean when a tidal wave generated by a tropical storm crashed over the cliff and pulled him into the churning waters. Witnesses said he had tried to swim back to shore but was unsuccessful. Several people on the beach finally were able to pull him from the water and worked to revive him, but it was too late. Stuart Alan Attman was 34 years old.

The story of Stuart's drowning became national news and was covered on NBC-TV's evening news program. The family's funeral for him had to be delayed until that Friday, November 18. Jamaican officials at first held up releasing his body to the family, even after Marc traveled to Jamaica to usher the body back to Baltimore. The Attmans eventually had to call on Congressman Ben Cardin and Congressman Kweisi Mfume for help. Mfume, who went on to head the NAACP and is now in private life, told me how difficult it was to deal with the authorities in Jamaica, but he pressed them on behalf of the Attman family. "Mfume really stepped in for us," Marc recalls. After several days of pressure from the two congressmen, the Jamaicans relented.

When the *Baltimore Sun* published its obituary on Stuart, they ran a picture taken previously in the store that showed Stuart and Seymour with their arms linked around each other's shoulder. Both are smiling warmly. Stuart, looking straight into the camera, is wearing a sweatshirt with "Attman's Delicatessen & Caterers of Lombard Street" emblazoned on the front. Seymour, dressed in tie and coat, is leaning his head toward his son and looking lovingly at him.

Indeed, there was much in their personalities that meshed and linked them. Both proved more interested and comfortable in the delicatessen business than in formal schooling or any of the professions. Both loved to banter with customers and employees. Debbie Attman, his sister-in-law, was quoted in the *Baltimore Jewish Times'* obituary as terming him "the mayor of Lombard Street." She added, "He just walked up to people and introduced himself. He had more friends than anybody I know." Earl G. Oppel, Jr., who has managed Attman's for more than 35 years and knew Stuart since he was a youngster, said he was "like a brother to everyone here and wasn't the typical boss' son."

Seymour, himself, was quoted as crediting his son's successful management of the catering side of Attman's to Stuart's love of people: "He knew everybody. He wanted to know everybody. He had the gift of gab and people loved his personality. He loved what he did and lived life to the fullest."

The same could certainly be said about Seymour.

Stuart's death was a mini-death for Seymour. Seymour renamed the Kibbitz Room the Stuart Attman Kibbitz Room to honor the memory of his youngest child. But the plan had been to leave the business to Stuart and that was now not possible. Those around Seymour began to see a less engaged and more subdued man. "It took away a lot of his zest for life," Marc remembers. "He never could accept Stuart's death."

Soon, Seymour began experiencing increased health issues. "He had been on a lot of pain medication from years of working 16 hours a day all his life," says Marc, who noted that his father would often work in the delicatessen's hot kitchen, which unlike the rest of the restaurant had no air-conditioning. He had high blood pressure and heart problems and in the 1980s had been taken by his brothers to a Milwaukee hospital which was then one of the few in the country specializing in heart bypass surgery. (Later, after his second wife died and he was informed he could no longer drive because of his poor health, the still-irrepressible Seymour Attman complained, "How am I going to date?")

With his realization that he should prepare for the next Attman generation to take over the delicatessen, Seymour began to talk to

Marc about becoming involved full-time. Although Marc, as many of the other Attmans, had helped out in the store as a youngster, he was a successful optometrist (he was a 1978 graduate of the Pennsylvania College of Optometry in Philadelphia) and since 1990 was co-owner of Sterling Optical, a string of 14 full-service optometry stores in the metro Baltimore and metro DC areas. At first, Marc was hesitant, remembering how his father had worked such long hours at the store. But his children and sisters pressed him to consider because, as he told me, they were all concerned about "continuing the legacy of the Attman's delicatessen."

He also realized how serious his father was about insuring the legacy of the family business when Seymour began revealing to him some of the secret recipes that Harry and Ida had developed and passed on to him, especially the seasonings in the recipes for corned beef, brisket, pastrami, and salami, and in the making of pickles: all of which Harry and Ida had made themselves. Ron Attman once remarked, only half in jest, that these recipes for the seasonings "seemed to be as closely guarded as the formula for Coca-Cola." (Those seasonings may be the reason why Rosemary Salconi, who grew up in Little Italy and is now in her 70s, told me her memory as an 11-year-old was eating an Attman's 25-cent corned beef on rye sandwich that was "like butter" and that she "has never had a sandwich like that.")

So in 2000, although he continued his involvement in Sterling Optical, Marc began working more closely with his father, immersing himself in the business of Attman's Delicatessen and bringing to its operations yet another Attman with entrepreneurial drive and experience. Marc was in the store in early June, 2002, when he saw

Seymour tell Earl Oppel, "If we have a good year next year, we'll put air-conditioning in the kitchen." Those were Seymour's last words. He took two steps and collapsed. Rushed to nearby Mercy Medical Center, Seymour lingered for three weeks, never regaining consciousness from a massive heart attack.

Because other Attmans were not able to devote the time to operating the store, Marc and his sisters took over responsibility for operations. Marc soon sold Sterling Optical and in 2003 opened Optical Fair in two Baltimore locations while at the same time spending more time overseeing Attman's Delicatessen. He now spends four to five days a week at the store and is on the phone daily with employees, suppliers or other business-related matters. He formally named Earl Oppel as director of operations and Dave Bush as assistant manager, both of whom have more than three decades of working at the delicatessen.

Marc sees his function is "to watch things like a hawk, to see what we buy and cook." While his father accumulated honors from such groups as Restaurant Association of Maryland and Hadassah and developed relationships with Maryland's elite (among Seymour's long-time good friends and patrons were Baltimore Orioles Jim Palmer and Brooks Robinson, with Cal Ripken making a visit after his playing days), Marc, in possibly an acknowledgement that few if anyone can duplicate the people-person abilities of his father, says he focuses himself on "running a profitable business and being nice to people."

And it seems to be working. The delicatessen now does a large mail order business and is experiencing 5% to 7% of its annual sales from the web, a figure that is growing. Plus the catering division continues to be successful. All of this is generated out of the same small space on Lombard Street. "The department stores wish they could do what we do per square foot," says Marc.

Consider, too, the following:

- The Food Channel has featured Attman's on its cable network.
- *USA Today* rated it among the top 10 delis in America.
- Attman's is listed as one of only 31 delis—and the only one from Maryland—in the book, *America's Great Delis.*
- *Southern* Magazine rated it the best deli in America.
- *Baltimore* Magazine named it the city's number one deli.
- Since 1975, the *City Paper's* reader survey has listed it the top deli.
- WJZ-TV airs a feature on the deli every Super Bowl weekend.
- Attman's is the largest food vendor at Ravens Stadium.
- The Ravens owner orders from Attman's for his suite for every home game.
- Attman's is the largest seller of corned beef in Maryland.
- Attman's sells the only private label brand of delicatessen outside of New York City.

In addition, Attman's is now immortalized in several best-selling books. Baltimore mystery writer Laura Lippman has set scenes in the Kibbitz Room. And famed novelist Tom Clancy has referred to the store in a number of his books. In fact, Clancy, who lives on the Eastern Shore and is the second largest shareholder in the Baltimore Orioles, is such a long-time fan of Attman's that he sends his private cook every three months to the store to buy delicatessen for himself or for parties. His purchases, according to Earl Oppel, are usually for several pounds of corned beef, pastrami, hot dogs, and a variety of other deli.

Marc and his sisters, who have witnessed all this interest and affection for the store, feel a special bond with it. They saw how devoted their father was to its operation, working every day and into the evenings. Although the conditions were demanding, Seymour would often say that "work is a joy" and tell his children and others, "Work and be happy." They remember how they would primarily see him for dinner only on Friday night for Sabbath meals. Otherwise, Seymour was at the delicatessen, where his father, Harry, had also worked into the evenings. This is why they could say, as they did when I met with Marc, Eileen, and Deborah to learn more about Seymour and Attman's Delicatessen: "We feel like it's our home." And each confirmed what one of them then said: "I feel my father and my grandfather there. I feel at peace."

Or as Marc remarked, echoing his late brother, Stuart, "There's an *Attmansphere* there."

As a result of Seymour's efforts—a combination of personality and perspiration—and the commitment by three generations of a family, Attman's today is the oldest family-operated delicatessen in America.

Chapter Six

"WE MANAGE TO PLEASE":
LEONARD PROVIDES HEALTH &
HOUSING FOR THOUSANDS

"I have a lot of respect for Leonard. He is a great community philanthropist. He's a leader because of his actions, not just words. If we had more Lennie Attmans around, we'd be a lot better in this country."

— Congressman C.A. Dutch Ruppersberger (Maryland – 2nd District) and former Baltimore County Executive

On the Sunday morning of December 14, 2008, just days before the holiday of Chanukah, the city of Annapolis is enwrapped in the invigorating feel of coming winter. The air is clear, crisp, and cold. As the historic capital of one of the original 13 colonies, Annapolis still has about it the look of early America. All of the government buildings clustered in the center of the city, even the newly-constructed, are built in the colonial style: neat rows of quiet red brick with wood trim painted white. Maryland's 250 year-old State House where the legislature meets is the oldest continually operated legislative building in America. Here is where George Washington came to resign his commission as head of the Continental Army, a first act before becoming president, and the public can still view the room where this significant event took place. Directly across from the State House, just past the path where Washington walked, is the Maryland Governor's official residence, called Government House, a stately three story colonial-style building.

It is here, in the home of the Governor, that Leonard Attman, the third child born in Maryland to immigrant parents from Eastern Europe, along with his wife, Phyllis, are today co-hosting a Chanukah party with the Governor and his wife. This is now an annual tradition after Leonard initiated it in 2003 when he suggested such festivities to the former governor, Robert Ehrlich, Jr. It is a tradition warmly embraced by the current governor, Martin O'Malley, after Leonard asked him if he would continue to host a Chanukah celebration. Sharing in the festivities this morning are a long list of guests, invited by the Attmans and the Governor, that include the Chief Judge of

Maryland's Special Court of Appeals, various state senators and delegates, Jewish legislators like Baltimore councilwoman Rikki Spector and U.S. Senator Ben Cardin. Also in attendance are a representative of the Israeli embassy and an array of friends and associates of Leonard and Phyllis, along with Ed and other Attman family members.

Upon arriving, guests are given green suede yarmulkes, donated by the Attmans, which have been inscribed with the state seal and the governor's name in Hebrew. Attendees are then ushered into the dining room where they find an elaborate Sunday brunch of catered kosher food. Here, too, because it is Chanukah, are generous helpings of latkes, the potato pancakes cooked in oil, which symbolize the miracle of Chanukah when a cruse of sacred oil containing a one-day supply burned in the Temple menorah for eight days until more oil could be made. In another room, the four-piece Kol Chayim Orchestra plays background music of Chanukah and Hebrew melodies. At the head of this room, resting on a pedestal, is a large hand-sculpted bronze menorah of nine dancing figures, each one holding a candle.

At a brief ceremony after the breakfast, Leonard thanks the governor and first lady for opening their home to host a celebration of the holiday of Chanukah. He also notes that the occasion marks the re-dedication of the menorah that he and his wife had commissioned for the governor's residence five years before when they learned it did not have a menorah to display during the holiday season. It was also a way, they felt, to mark their 50th anniversary five years before and now appropriately being re-dedicated on their 55th anniversary.

But this particular menorah is especially meaningful. Phyllis had commissioned the artist, Zachary Oxman, a prize-winning

Maryland-based sculptor who is in the audience this day, to recreate the menorah he had first fashioned for the White House Collection of American Crafts. That menorah is presently on display in the Clinton Presidential Center in Little Rock, Arkansas. Leonard tells the assembled guests, "Our re-dedication of this menorah reflects our Attman family's treasured friendship with Governor Martin O'Malley and Katie because of their warmth and respect of our Jewish heritage and caring for our well-being throughout the state. Governor O'Malley is a valued true friend to all of us here and we thank his family for showing all future generations of visitors that the miracle of Chanukah will always glow in Government House."

Leonard then calls on Rabbi Ronald Shulman, spiritual leader of Chizuk Amuno Congregation, to explain the tradition and symbolism of Chanukah and to preside over the lighting of the menorah candles by selected honored guests. After the candles are lit, Governor O'Malley, wearing a navy blue tie with 'Shalom' repeated on it in yellow, and with his wife and children by his side, speaks briefly but movingly. He notes that George Washington said that three things get a person through tough times: "courage, faith, and hope." "This," he says, "is also the message of Chanukah."

Leonard and Phyllis present personal gifts to the O'Malleys and their children, including a bronze kiddush cup they commissioned Zachary Oxman to create. It shows a man in old world garb joyously celebrating.

In remarks about the kiddush cup that could be said about the special menorah being re-dedicated, Leonard continues: "Zachary's sculpture captures those fleeting moments that define us: our love of family, our joy in music and our hopes for the future. Zachary's passion has been to create art that elevates the spirit and it certainly elevates mine." Leonard concludes by raising the cup to the Governor and his family and reciting the blessing over wine in Hebrew, ending with, "L'Chaim, to Life!"

Senator Cardin also speaks, thanking the Governor and the Attmans for "making a reality of the openness of Maryland to the people of the Jewish faith."

The program concludes with Rabbi Stuart Weinblatt of Bnai Tzedek Congregation in Potomac, Maryland, pointing out that a menorah "banishes darkness" and that this has been the Jewish role, "to bring light to the world." He also acknowledges how the Attmans strive to do this by fostering these and similar events. "Massachusetts has the Kennedys. Maryland has the Attmans. It's quite a dynasty," the rabbi declares.

Leonard Attman was named for his mother's brother who was killed in a pogrom in Europe just months before he was scheduled to leave for America. On this morning in the Governor's residence, Leonard showed how far the Attmans and indeed American Jewry have come from those days of dread in Europe. In a previous interview for a show about Jewish Americans aired on Comcast cable television, he lovingly recalled growing up in East Baltimore amid the Jewish community that then thrived along the Lombard Street corridor, from Patterson Park down to Lloyd Street. He remembered the closeness of the Jewish youth of the day and how they would gather on the steps of houses or at a drug store soda fountain to meet and talk. He recalled that there were parties where everyone was friendly with no exclusive dating, doctors readily made house calls, doors would be left unlocked day or night without worry, he and others were welcomed into the homes and stores of the Italian and Polish communities as their members were welcomed into Jewish homes and stores, how at least a dozen synagogues were within walking distance along Baltimore Street and various side roads, and how everyone dressed in their finest for the Jewish holidays and would know and greet each other as they strolled along the street.

In an especially memorable passage, he talked about the "flavor and the aroma" of the cooking and baking that emanated from the Jewish homes as he walked by on the holidays. "You wanted to sort of knock on the door, go inside and get a piece of mandel bread or a piece of kichel that one of the grandmothers was making or one of the parents were making in the house." He cited "the aroma of the gefilte fish that was being cooked" and how it reminded him of "the absolute feeling of being in your own community. It was like you could be ten blocks away, but you felt like you were in your own house just by being near to the people that were dear to each other and their family life and dear to the community to stay together and help each other in need. That gave us the flavor of knowing that we were in a safe and wonderful environment in the wonderful land of America."

One institution that stood out in Leonard's reminiscences of growing up was the JEA (Jewish Educational Alliance), a four-story facility located on Baltimore Street near Central Avenue which provided a gathering place and focus of activities for Jewish teenagers and young adults. Here they engaged in various recreational sports like basketball, track and field, and wrestling matches; played ping pong; enjoyed arts and crafts; and formed debating teams.

"The JEA afforded us the ability to learn how to get together and work together in groups," he recalled. He noted that there were 20 to 30 different clubs active at the JEA, with formations of basketball and softball leagues, track and field meets, and ping pong and debating tournaments. And eventually, the JEA hosted dances and social get-togethers.

Leonard was an active participant in much of this and formed friendships that have lasted ever since. JEA reunions have been held annually over the years, with up to 500 people attending. Leonard has been one of those who have been honored at these reunions, whether for working at the JEA, participating in a JEA activity, or going on to be successful in the community. He pointed out that even 60 years later he was still receiving a call from the JEA president wishing him a happy birthday or happy anniversary. "It's a warm feeling to know that there are people who care as much about you today as cared about you then. That's a unique quality that our Jewish community put together at that time."

Another institution that helped form Leonard was the Talmudical Academy of Baltimore (TA), the first Hebrew day school in America founded outside of New York City. "My mother insisted on education, primarily Jewish education," Leonard says. He attended the school from kindergarten through high school, graduating in one of the school's early twelfth grades. Here, combined with his growing up in a traditional Jewish home, he received his grounding in Judaism, which fostered his life-long love for the Jewish faith and commitment to Jewish and other philanthropic causes. TA also offered him another benefit: a special thought process.

"TA taught me, through Talmudic study, how to think deeper, how to analyze every situation you're in: social, political, religious or monetary. It gave me the best part of how I conduct myself in life. It was absolutely phenomenal. To this day, I always credit TA for this."

Interestingly, at Talmudical Academy he also had the opportunity to show his athletic skill. Ray Casper, a blind older gentleman who was a good friend of Leonard's father and a supporter of the school, knew of Leonard's abilities as a basketball player. One day, he told Leonard that he would fund a basketball team for the school if Leonard would help put together a team good enough to compete with other schools. Leonard took up the challenge.

"We had no gym to practice in, so the school let us go one day a week on an early Friday afternoon to the YMHA, Young Men's Hebrew Association, which is today called the Jewish Community Center," he recalled. "We put together a team and got accepted into the junior varsity league for private schools. We played such schools as Towson Catholic, Gilman, Mount St. Joe, and Park School. We even played some public schools as well."

Some of TA's games were played as preliminary games for the Baltimore Bullets, who at the time was the city's professional team playing in the Coliseum, then on Monroe Street.

"Having a Jewish team compete with the non-Jewish community gave us a lot of pride."

The last year that Leonard attended TA, before he graduated and went to college, he led his team to victory in every game they played and won the league championship. "We were very, very proud of ourselves."

Another lasting influence on Leonard growing up was his home life. Although his father worked 12 to 14 hours a day, his father and mother created a close-knit environment for their children. The family always ate dinner together and observed the Sabbath. Leonard would attend synagogue with his father, remembering still "the transmission of warmth in holding my father's hand" as they walked to and from services. Among the elements of shared family life, Leonard still cherishes how he became enthralled with Jewish music when his parents played records of Jewish music and cantorial performances. "Cantors then were real 'baal tfilos,'" he remembers, using the Hebrew term for leaders of prayer. "In the synagogue, during the cantor's singing, you could hear the whimpers and cries of the women in the gallery. That transmission of feeling is few and far between today." But that experience had its effect, with Leonard himself becoming an adept singer and leader of congregational prayer.

Another life-long practice he learned during his early years, along with his brothers, was to dress appropriately for the occasion. "Our pride in wanting to dress nicely comes from our mother, who was known for being an elegant dresser."

The parents also imparted a strong feeling for charity. Leonard vividly remembers the many charity boxes maintained in the home for different organizations not only in Baltimore, but also in such other locales as Cleveland, Milwaukee, New York and Israel. He especially remembers how his mother and father would donate in increments of 18 and 36, which have the same numerical value as in the Hebrew words for "life." Back then his struggling parents made their denominations in cents (his mother would deposit pennies, nickels and dimes in various donation boxes before lighting the Sabbath candles), but today Leonard and his brothers will give in multiples of 18 and 36 dollars; at times, in hundreds, thousands or more. "We learned to give in those denominations."

Leonard remembers, too, as does Edward, how those small donations of his parents came back to help the family, of how when Seymour became sick and needed to go to a hospital in Milwaukee for a heart operation, a rabbi there who twice yearly visited the deli to collect donations from the Attmans responded by warmly welcoming Leonard and Edward, providing them with lodging and prayers of support. The rabbi also visited Seymour daily in the hospital. "We were in dire need of hope and prayer for Seymour's recovery. This was a very unique experience. It shows what can happen as a Jewish family expands beyond its own" and reaches out to other Jews and other people, Leonard notes.

Indeed, the charitable impulse runs deep in the Attmans because of what Ida and Harry transmitted to their children. "I still remember being told that the money you make you are only a temporary trustee of, that you are meant to do good things with it."

He recounts how his mother would give him change to give to poor people selling pencils in front of Baltimore's downtown department stores during the Depression. She would tell him to give the money but not take the pencils. He saw his father giving food to individuals who were inebriated and who had come into the store looking for a handout, providing them with bread, a piece of meat, and a pickle.

The existence of the deli itself provided a deep and lasting influence on Leonard and his brothers in a way that would help them in their later business lives. In addition to providing them with work experience and an ethic of hard work (Leonard worked the cash register and like Seymour learned to count change in various languages), the deli introduced the boys to all types of individuals.

"We felt very lucky that our parents had a store. Here we could meet people of different ethnic groups, of any race or creed, and had a chance to interact with them. It gave us the ability to talk to people at any level at any time." That exposure, Leonard believes, enabled him and his siblings to easily make contacts and friendships with others and conduct their future business dealings in an open, congenial manner. "Whatever success I've achieved, it is primarily due to the way my father and mother set up the store."

After Leonard graduated high school, he went to the University of Maryland at College Park. It was there, during their first year in college, that he and his future wife initially met.

Phyllis Lazinsky was born in Baltimore on October 7, 1933, the daughter of Rose and Joseph Lazinsky. Rose's father, like Leonard's parents and his parents' family, was from Eastern Europe. Born in Russia, Joseph was brought to the United States at the age of two by his parents, Sarah and Morris Lazinsky. Phyllis's mother, Rose, was born in the United States to Joseph and Sarah Delsen. Phyllis's younger sister, Harriet, as well as her mother's brother and two sisters, were all born in Baltimore.

Leonard and Phyllis saw each other for the first time at the University of Maryland's Hillel House, a gathering place for Jewish students sponsored by the B'nai B'rith Youth Organization on various college campuses. After graduating from Forest Park High School (Class of '52), she was attending UM for pre-nursing and Leonard was studying pre-law.

"I don't know how we were attracted to each other. We just

started talking," Phyllis recalls more than 50 years later.

The two would often meet to continue their conversations at the nearby Hot Shoppe, where they found themselves growing closer while enjoying together their mutual favorite—hot fudge ice cream and cake. The relationship quickly deepened over the ensuing months.

"It was like when people say you find your beshert (intended) you know it. I feel it is chemistry people feel to each other. It's not looks. You either click or you don't. We have still today as wonderful a time alone with each other as when we are with other people, because we think a lot alike," says Phyllis. She notes that they love the same things, such as the theater and music (especially opera, pop, and Streisand). "The only thing we disagree about is art. I like strong, realistic art, while Leonard prefers impressionistic works, sculptures, and watercolors."

After dating for nearly a year, on December 15, 1953, they married. Rabbi Samuel Rosenblatt of Beth Tfiloh, where Phyllis's parents were members, along with Rabbis Vitsick and Perlmutter, performed the ceremony. (Noting that three rabbis officiated, Leonard quips, "I guess my parents wanted to make certain the wedding was kosher.") Leonard was 19, Phyllis was 20.

"Leonard's mother was very much in favor of Leonard marrying young," Phyllis says. In characteristic fashion, Ida said she wanted Leonard to get married "when he was young and foolish" rather than, by waiting, do something unwise in the interim.

"For us it worked," says Phyllis, noting that at the time of our interview they had been married for 56 years. Leonard, in a separate interview, remarked, "I was lucky enough to get married to her."

After marriage, Leonard transferred from the University of

Maryland at College Park to the University of Baltimore, taking night courses while working during the day. He first worked for Crown Realty, a real estate company owned by Phyllis's father and Albert Kishter, who became a life-long mentor to Leonard in real estate. Leonard would collect ground rents from downtown properties owned by his father-in-law. The couple's first residence was in the Hilton Village apartments and Leonard was making $60 a week. Phyllis remembers that "sometimes we had difficulty making the rent" and she offered to get a job. But Leonard did not want her to go to work, a difference that led to what Phyllis says was "our only big fight in our married life."

Over the years, Phyllis, with several friends as partners, would operate three successful businesses: the Green Door, a junior dress shop; Hands of Man, featuring crafted items from artists around the country; and the Signature Collection, offering hand-painted individualized gifts (the store, in which Phyllis employed two artists full-time, proved so successful it attracted much media attention, with The Baltimore Sun and various magazines publishing articles about its unique operation).

Interestingly, while Phyllis loves crafts and built two businesses around it, she acknowledges that she herself "can't do a thing art wise." She points out that their daughter Shellye is the artist, painting in oil and watercolor. However, Phyllis loves to cook and bake, and notes that her mother and Leonard's mother were "both wonderful at cooking and baking." Ida shared with Phyllis many of her recipes, which Phyllis still uses, especially Ida's honey cake.

The couple eventually moved to Clarks Lane apartments where Phyllis became pregnant with their first child, Shellye, born January

25, 1956. The next move was to a home on Labyrinth Road. Edward and Seymour had homes there, beginning a family tradition of the brothers living near each other. During these years, Jeffrey was born (July 26, 1961) and then another daughter, Wende (April 21, 1963). Today, Leonard and Phyllis live in a community off of Stevenson Road (near where Edward and Mildred also live). Located near their synagogue, Chizuk Amuno, Leonard and Phyllis's home is filled with art, books, family pictures, and Judaica, including a smaller version of the Oxman-designed Chanukah menorah that they donated to the Governor's residence. They presently have nine grandchildren.

For both Leonard and Phyllis, these decades have been filled with many business enterprises and civic and philanthropic endeavors. Five years after working for Crown Realty, Leonard, exhibiting the entrepreneurial spirit of the Attmans, launched his own business, a real estate development company. A keen observer, he had acquired a knowledge of real estate and construction that he has constantly added to throughout his professional life. One family member has termed him a "font of information and a lifelong learner." Liking the housing industry, he initially focused on building single family homes. He realized that in those days people were beginning to move out of Baltimore City and into suburbia and that much of Anne Arundel County, with the Baltimore Beltway yet to be built, was not fully developed. He was advised that properties purchased near Ritchie Highway and in the Glen Burnie area would eventually become valuable. So the first project he undertook was to build houses in Glen Burnie. His selling price: $9900, with washer/dryer included.

His first foray into apartments came in the 1960s with the development of Severn Square, with his brother Edward as a partner.

He also built the first luxury condominium apartment building in Baltimore, Strathmore Towers on Park Heights Avenue. To adorn the building, he placed a stone sculpture out front that had been displayed at the World's Fair held in New York and that Leonard's father had purchased as a gift.

(One early building project Leonard undertook was for his father, transforming a garage attached to Seymour's house on Northbrook Road into an apartment for Harry after Ida passed away. This enabled the brothers, along with their father, to live near each other.)

Leonard's enterprises have always been marked by flair and creativity, along with soundness in design.

"My father is an expert marketer," says Shellye. "He's a true visionary who follows his instincts. He's very creative with amazing ideas. Dad is someone who likes to think outside the box. He does not follow convention and is always trying to find that 'extra something.'"

Shellye points out that he would go to Philadelphia to see which developers were selling out their properties. He would take his children to his own projects, asking them what they did or did not like, and then explaining why someone would prefer one property and not another. "It was fun to look at houses," says Wende.

Soon, Leonard formed a partnership with Albert Kishter, who had played a particularly meaningful role in Leonard's career as a developer. In the early stages of the company, Leonard invited his brother-in-law, Lowell Glazer, who was married to Phyllis's sister, Harriet, to join the company. Lowell had been working with Phyllis's father in Crown Realty.

The result, in 1968, was the formation of A&G Management Co., Inc., which eventually came to build, manage and maintain apartment communities throughout Anne Arundel, Baltimore and Howard Counties. Today, the company owns and oversees more than 3,000 one-, two-, and three-bedroom units ranging from garden apartments to townhomes to adult luxury apartment communities. Leonard's companies have grown to own, manage and lease 14 apartment and townhome communities. They include apartments named Bay Hills, Chapel Manor, Park East, Colonial Square, Severn Square, Stage Coach, Olde Stage, Overbrook, Oak Ridge, and Plumtree. Developments with both apartments and townhomes are Northbrooke Township and Southgate. There is also an adult luxury apartment community named the Islands of FoxChase. The company's corporate slogan for developing and overseeing these properties: "We Manage to Please."

All of this—including Leonard's establishment in 1986 of Attman Properties Company to build and manage what is now 1.2 million square feet of commercial, office, retail and industrial properties in and around Maryland—has resulted in Leonard creating one of the Mid-Atlantic's significant real estate development enterprises.

Leonard also applied his entrepreneurial zeal to another of his interests—food—creating a series of confectionery shops called The Great Cookie, which operated for decades. Pointing to her father's willingness to try new things as a major factor in his success, Shellye points out, "You have to be a bit of a gambler and willing to take calculated risks. My Dad will take those risks. He is entrepreneurial and adventurous. Much of these traits are inherent in him, and I'm sure many he also learned from his parents and his roots."

Another business risk that Leonard took and has proved highly successful involved a new area for him—nursing homes—and a partnership with his nephew, Gary.

That partnership seems to have been a long-time in the making. Gary's mother was pregnant with him when she served as a bridesmaid at Leonard and Phyllis's wedding, and when he was born he became Leonard and Phyllis's godson. Leonard also helped Gary obtain his coveted appointment as a congressional page in Washington during high school.

As a lawyer with also a CPA degree, Gary, after joining the law firm of Gordon Feinblatt, had developed his own practice, representing numerous nursing and healthcare facilities. Interestingly, he first entered this field through contacts provided by Acme Paper, which has numerous nursing home clients. Gary's contacts now help Acme acquire other customers.

Utilizing his experience with the nursing and healthcare field, Gary suggested to Leonard that they look into an opportunity that arose when three city-based facilities became available. That situation did not work out, says Gary, because the seller changed her mind at the last minute. But the experience led the two of them to establish a business model that they felt would work with any future opportunities. Looking back now, Gary says, "Sometimes the best deal you do is the deal you don't do."

That promising opportunity arose in 1986 when Gary learned of a nursing home under construction in Clinton, Maryland. He brought the situation to Leonard's attention and proposed the possibility that the two of them, drawing on their different experiences and skills, could purchase and operate the facility successfully. After considering the proposal, Leonard agreed and secured the financing, Gary and Leonard negotiated the deal, and they brought in Alvin Powers as another partner to manage the home. Shortly thereafter, Leonard's son, Jeffrey, joined the company as a member of the leadership team.

That was the beginning of further investments in nursing homes and the formation of their company, FutureCare Health and Management Corporation, for Gary had another client who owned nursing homes but was in poor health and looking to sell. The sale came with a certificate of need to build two more nursing homes. FutureCare and its affiliates then started acquiring other homes, especially those with good real estate but poor management. And because of Leonard's close working relationship with the banks and the emerging respect FutureCare was creating in the industry, the company was able to obtain the financing needed to pursue other opportunities as they appeared.

"No one else in our market could do what we could do. We had a unique combination of skills comprising expertise in local real estate, construction, operations, and financial, and we were very entrepreneurial," says Gary. Besides, he notes, "In this business, we serve the public good by turning lemons, underperforming nursing homes operated by others, into lemonade."

Among some of the properties the company acquired and transformed were the former North Charles Street Hospital, which was renamed as FutureCare Homewood; a city-owned facility in the poor area of Sandtown/Winchester; and physically outstanding but previously under-performing nursing homes in Irvington and Charles Village. Another purchase, in the Lochearn area, proved to be unique. It was a nursing home originally utilized as the Villa St. Michael Convent. This "amazing structure," says Gary, came with pews, confession booths, a marble altar, 30-foot high-coffered and vaulted ceilings, and 13 stained glass windows, each a story tall. With this purchase, the Attman family, just two generations removed from its Eastern European Jewish roots, now owned a church and former convent!

Over the past 27 years, with Leonard contributing his business acumen, knowledge of construction, and access to funding; Gary, with his background in law and accounting, providing the operational and financial oversight; and with Leonard's son Jeffrey, who joined the company shortly after its inception, serving as senior vice president and focusing on construction and operations, FutureCare has grown to own and operate 12 comprehensive short- and long-term nursing and rehabilitation facilities in the Baltimore/Washington area. The company now serves approximately 1800 patients and employs more than 2700 people. Leonard notes that this is "a larger operation than any hospital around." Indeed, many hospitals send them patients of all ages for therapy, rehabilitation, and long-term care. The company also has a homecare division to serve the elderly and handicapped living at home, and its principals are investors in an ambulance company. Today, FutureCare is the nation's 40th largest nursing home chain, with plans to grow further.

To explain the company's success, one can see various keys to its operation. They bought at a price that made financial sense, passing on many deals that did not fit their business model. They adopted a long-term strategy, sticking with a project and willing to wait over time to turn it around ("Lennie is a very patient person"). They didn't take on more projects than they could handle at a time. And the owners are not afraid to hear and deal with bad news (Gary remembers how after working with his uncle for a month, Leonard told him, "If you're not making mistakes, you're not doing enough"). Indeed, Gary says that in working with his uncle he often "learned in one day what I learned in a semester in college." Above all, for Gary, what Leonard taught him could be encapsulated in one concept: "We only want facilities on which we're proud to have our family name."

To Phyllis, Leonard's success—and that of the Attman family—comes down to two elements. One is "hard work." The other is "having good people to work with across the board. When people get along, businesses are successful."

Shellye also notes that some of Leonard's business success comes from the fact that everything her father builds is owner-managed, giving him a handle on operations. And she too alludes to the fact that the Attmans are involved as a family and the public likes that: "as long as people know there is a family behind the name, customers feel part of the family." Indeed, five members of the Attman family are now active in Leonard's various entities, with him serving as chairman. In addition to Gary and Jeffrey with FutureCare, Shellye plays a leadership role in the family's residential and commercial real estate operations, serving as president of A&G Management and vice president of Attman Properties; Wende is vice president of both companies; and Jeffrey, as he is with FutureCare, is also vice president of Attman Properties, responsible among his various duties for construction and maintenance operations. Even the next generation is now involved, with granddaughter Rebecca recently joining the staff. As Shellye says, for the Attmans, "family comes before business."

Leonard himself credits his parents and the values they instilled. "Whatever success I've achieved primarily comes from the way I saw my father and mother conduct their store." He vividly remembers how, during difficult times in the 1930s, rather than declare bankruptcy, his father worked over the years to repay $50,000 in debts he owed to various people. This lesson, he says, has guided him in his dealings with banks and customers: the importance of being "a person of your word."

As a person, Leonard is very much in his own mold. Not only does he think "outside the box" as his daughter notes, but he is not confined to being easily categorized. Without formal training in math, engineering or architecture, he quickly learned the math necessary to assess the feasibility of investing in and building apartments, homes, and health care facilities. He is full of energy, "a man with so many interests," says Gary; a person, says Shellye, "who does everything with passion." Like his mother, he is a smart and colorful dresser, known for favoring bright sport coats. He plays golf and bridge, and travels the world extensively with Phyllis ("the only things we don't do are castles and rain forests," she says). Like other Attmans, he loves spectator sports and has box seats for football, baseball and basketball. Continuing an interest he showed in his young years at the Talmudical Academy, he also enjoys learning and attends Jewish classes.

But he always finds time for family, for his children and grandchildren, and for the extended Attman family. At the age of 75, he bought an IPhone and learned how to text message so that he could keep in close contact with his grandchildren. His niece, Lisa, remembers that during the six years she was living in New York City, whenever Leonard brought his children to see a Broadway show, he would invite her to join them, a memory she still cherishes. His nephews still talk of visiting his home as youngsters and delighting in finding a pinball machine and player piano that he put at their disposal.

Indeed, in referring to Leonard, Attman family members use words like gregarious, warm, energetic, generous, colorful, and creative. He would use all of these attributes to maximize another word said of him: philanthropic.

Helping found a school for youngsters diagnosed with dyslexia… serving on the board of an African-American heritage museum… supporting the synagogue at the Naval Academy…contributing to the planting of thousands of trees in the Land of Israel…promoting the heritage of Jewish music…organizing major fund raisers featuring internationally-known entertainers, United States senators and the U.S. Secretary of State.

These are just some of the ways that Leonard's energetic touch has been expressed in behalf of an array of organizations and causes. As with his parents and his brothers, Leonard and his immediate family are known not only by their business activities, but also by their broad civic and philanthropic involvements that have helped countless individuals and institutions.

In 1966, it was brought to Leonard and Phyllis's attention that bright and energetic children can have learning problems due to dyslexia, which causes reading difficulties but is not associated with a person's mental capacity. When Leonard and Phyllis soon realized that no school existed to teach such children but that David Malin, a specialist in the field, was looking to head such a school "because of the terrible need," the Attmans went about raising money and helping launch what became the Jemicy School. Founded in 1973, the school is geared to "bright students struggling with dyslexia or other language-based learning differences by addressing their intellectual strengths and their learning needs."

Starting with a small group of students in a house donated by former County Councilman Mickey Miller, Jemicy today serves 270 students, ages 6 to 18, with 73 faculty members operating on two locations in Owings Mills with a lower school on a 23-acre campus and a middle/upper school on a 57-acre campus.

Phyllis, herself, is dyslexic. She remembers her elementary school teacher working with her to write the 'p' in her name forwards rather than backwards, a sign of dyslexia. Another sign: at a wedding reception, she once read the place card as indicating table number 9 rather than the correct table 6, and after she and Leonard spent most of the evening in the wrong seats, Leonard now checks the place cards.

"The shame is that kids with dyslexia have to struggle when with the right teaching approach they can do well," Phyllis says, pointing out that Jemicy uses these specialized methods, which the public schools don't.

"These are all bright kids. Lawyers and doctors have graduated from Jemicy. Many have gone on to private high schools where they have been on honor rolls and some have graduated cum laude from college," she says.

"We feel Jemicy is a wonderful achievement. Today, they can't handle all those who apply. It wouldn't be here if we didn't push for this kind of school."

Among his many other civic activities, Leonard served for five years as president of the Baltimore region of the Jewish National Fund and has been on its executive committee for more than 20 years, has been treasurer of Sinai Hospital, has served on the board of the State's Drug Abuse Authority, has chaired events for the Talmudical Academy of Baltimore, has co-chaired with attorney Philip Altfeld an American Cancer Society benefit honoring then-Maryland's Attorney General Francis 'Bill' Burch, and has chaired sell-out events for the Retinitis Pigmentosa Foundation that featured opera star Beverly Sills and country singer Kenny Rogers and that honored noted Baltimoreans Shoshana and Jerry Cardin.

He sits on the board of the University of Maryland Shock Trauma Center, which is the nation's first trauma hospital; is the only Jew serving on the board of the Reginald F. Lewis Museum that is devoted to African American history and culture; and was appointed by former Republican Governor Robert Ehrlich, Jr., and then reappointed by Democratic Governor Martin O'Malley to a 4-year term on the Maryland Stadium Authority, which oversees Oriole Park at Camden Yards and M&T Stadium where the Baltimore Ravens play. In 2013, Governor O'Malley reappointed Leonard yet again to the Stadium Authority, the only time anyone had ever served three terms under two different governors.

But Leonard not only attends Stadium Authority meetings and votes on issues, he offers insights and ideas that have made a difference. As the only one on the Authority with real estate experience, he has saved the state considerable sums of money, especially with his review of the leasing of parking operations.

As a 10-year member of the board of the Shock Trauma Center, he co-chaired in 2010 its annual Shock Trauma Gala, a major fundraiser for the Center. He is also an active participant in a $35 million three-year fund raising program, which is an integral part of a $150 million federally-funded expansion of Shock Trauma arranged by Congressmen C.A. Dutch Ruppersberger and Elijah Cummings.

Said Congressman Ruppersberger, who helped create the Shock Trauma Center after his life was literally saved by trauma specialist Dr. R Adams Cowley following an accident: "I have a lot of respect for Leonard. He is a great community philanthropist, a very warm, generous, quality person. With Shock Trauma, he is always there to do what he can. He is a leader because of his actions, not just words. If we had more Lennie Attmans around, we'd be a lot better in this country."

And in advising the black heritage Reginald F. Lewis Museum, located on the eastside of downtown, on the need to reach out to a wider audience, Leonard linked up the museum with Rabbi Shlomo Porter, executive director of the Etz Chaim Center for Jewish Living and Learning, who had asked for advice where the Center could hold night-time adult education classes for Jews living or working downtown. The result was a successful arrangement between the museum and Etz Chaim in which Jewish attendees learned at sessions conducted in the museum's meeting rooms.

"I had met Leonard when he and his wife had donated the funds for the lobby in our new building, and because of his knowledge of real estate and his connections, I thought he would know where we could find space for a new program we wanted to start in the downtown area," Rabbi Porter recalled. "What he suggested seemed 'out of the box,' but it proved very, very successful."

The new program, which was geared for Jews of all backgrounds, attracted Jewish college students and young professionals, as well as seniors. It ran for two years with nearly fifty people—twice as many as expected—joining together for supper and learning. "It was quite a thing to see: Jews eating kosher Chinese food, drinking Mexican beer, and learning about Judaism in a museum devoted to the the heritage of African-Americans," said Rabbi Porter, with a smile.

Among other Jewish institutions he is associated with are Beth Tfiloh Congregation, an Orthodox synagogue, and Chizuk Amuno Congregation, which is Conservative. Leonard first joined Beth Tfiloh when he married Phyllis, whose family were members. He would attend services on the Sabbath and on the holidays and many times would be honored with singing the haftorah, the portion recited after the weekly reading from the Torah. He sent his daughter Shellye to its day school and today serves on the synagogue's board of directors and on its religious committee. Recently, in response to a need to motivate more people to attend Selihos services, which are held at midnight at the beginning of the High Holiday period, he suggested the shul invite the daughter of the late singer Shlomo Carlebach to perform. The result was a large turnout of college youth and a "very powerful and wonderful evening."

Shellye's husband, Steve, previously served as chairman of Beth Tfiloh's board, and in 2010 the synagogue honored the family at its Community Day School's annual Spotlight event, with Shellye and Steve serving as co-chairs and Wende and Jeffrey heading up various phases of the evening. In response, Leonard and Phyllis created a scholarship fund for Beth Tfiloh's day school.

"Lennie and Phyllis have been linked to Beth Tfiloh for several generations," notes Rabbi Mitchell Wohlberg, the synagogue's spiritual leader. "The Attman connection goes back to Phyllis's parents, who were members. And Phyllis's mother, Rose, at 101 is our oldest member. And not only were Lennie and Phyllis married by our Rabbi Rosenblatt, but their daughter and granddaughter were married here."

In noting the involvements of Leonard's children, son-in-law and grandchildren in Beth Tfiloh, Rabbi Wohlberg expressed appreciation for how Leonard "would always be there to help with different projects, especially to help with a haftorah."

"Lennie knows how to do a haftorah well," says Rabbi Wohlberg. "In fact, Lennie is the last of a dying breed: He loves rabbis and cantors."

Rabbi Wohlberg has a special fondness for Leonard for another reason. As he points out in his humorous way, "We share something in common. We are both from well-known families, we are both the third son, and we are both the last child. But Lennie went on to make something of himself."

As a demonstration of Leonard's broad interest in supporting Jewish causes and institutions, he also joins with other Attman family members in belonging to and attending services at Chizuk Amuno, often alternating between Chizuk Amuno and Beth Tfiloh, especially on holidays. Here too, he and Phyllis have made a significant mark on the growth and activities of Chizuk Amuno. Says Chizuk Amuno's Rabbi Ronald Shulman, "Lennie likes to think big. He is a devoted member who generously provides resources for special congregational efforts and needs."

One such offering Rabbi Shulman cites: "Each fall, the community enjoys Sukkot in the Attman Family Sukkah, a structure that stands in our courtyard due to the creative thinking of Lennie and the entire Attman family."

Rabbi Shulman points out that "Leonard is very proud of the Jewish heritage he was raised to appreciate. He savors good cantorial music and the richness of Jewish culture. It has been Lennie's sincere desire to share these passions with the Chizuk Amuno Community whenever possible."

Leonard not only participates in the work of civic and charitable organizations, but, in keeping with his creative approaches to life, often seeks to contribute in ways that are different. "I try to do things that are unique," he says.

-- Such as on his 50th wedding anniversary, dedicating with Phyllis all of the prayer books and Hebrew bibles to the new Naval Academy synagogue in Annapolis.

-- Such as on his 75th birthday, donating to 75 different charities.

-- Such as supporting, for the past 12 years, the JNF's B'nai Mitzvah Program in which a tree is planted for every bar and bat mitzvah taking place in Baltimore City and Baltimore and Howard Counties, a number of trees that now runs into several thousands and that has resulted in Leonard and Phyllis being part of planting a forest of trees in the American Independence Park in the hills of Jerusalem. "This is a fabulous way to instill Zionist feelings into the next generation," says Diane Scar, JNF's Mid-Atlantic Zone Director. "When kids see this, they feel a part of Israel because of the Attman family."

Adds Diane: "We really love Leonard and Phyllis and the entire Attman family. This is truly a family that makes things happen."

-- Such as creating, with the input of Chizuk Amuno's then Rabbi Joel Zaiman and Director Stanley Minch, a Simhah Display Wall in the synagogue's lobby where Jewish art objects are on permanent display, with others to be added periodically.

-- Such as establishing the Phyllis and Leonard Attman Program Fund for Jewish Music and Cultural Arts to "perpetuate our rich heritage of Jewish music in synagogues, schools, and homes." This continues Leonard's childhood enthrallment with Jewish music when he listened to his parents' records of Jewish music and cantorial singing and when he heard the cantors in his youth perform so movingly. Chizuk Amuno serves as the home to the fund, which seeks to foster Jewish identity by bringing not only classical Jewish music but all Jewish cultural expression to the larger Baltimore Jewish community. The Attmans committed $100,000 over four years to the project.

-- Such as, in celebration of his 50th wedding anniversary and his 70th birthday, on October 9, 2003, sponsoring a special concert at Chizuk Amuno of three noted cantors, each from the Orthodox, Conservative and Reform branches of Judaism. A capacity crowd of several thousand people attended to hear Cantors Avi Albrecht of Beth Tfiloh, Emanuel Perlman of Chizuk Amuno, and Melvin Luterman of Oheb Shalom sing, accompanied by the Baltimore Symphony Orchestra. To his knowledge, Leonard says, this was the first time that cantors from the three branches of Judaism had performed on the same program, but that is what he intended. "I wanted a mixture of Orthodox, Conservative and Reform to bring the community together."

Leonard's office houses the artifacts of his personal, professional and philanthropic life. Here are pictures of him with his brothers, pictures of his wife and family. Here are the plaques and mementos signifying an active, involved individual. But several of those photos represent stories that tell how Leonard, the youngest of the first Attman generation to grow up in America, epitomizes the place and role of the Attmans in today's world.

One picture shows the Attman brothers with then-Secretary of State Henry Kissinger. Another picture is of Leonard and his children with the late Senator Edward Kennedy when he was an active member of the United States Senate. A third picture is of Leonard and Governor Marvin Mandel with former Vice President Hubert Humphrey. The photos were taken in the mid-1970s when Leonard was for two years banquet chairman followed by two years as president of the Chizuk Amuno Congregation Brotherhood and brought such notables to Baltimore to be honored at the brotherhood's Donor Dinners, a major source of funding for the synagogue.

"As I became involved in the brotherhood, I wanted to do something special so we could raise significant sums for our congregation's educational and youth programs," he says as he shows me the pictures.

First, he launched what was termed "Festival of Stars," in which a series of variety shows with high-profile entertainers were featured to attract large audiences. Then, he shifted to honoring national and international political figures. "These were unique events at a time when organizations and synagogues didn't think of doing this. When you get to a saturation point, you need to put a new twist on things. This then raises awareness of a cause and the money follows."

Leonard began by bringing to Baltimore the pianist/entertainer

Liberace. The following years he brought in such noted performers as Jimmy Durante, Alan King, and Carmen Caballero.

Then, utilizing his contacts in politics and government, he initially arranged for Hubert Humphrey as the former vice president to be honored at a donor dinner. The following year he arranged for Governor Mandel to be an honoree. Following that, he set his sights on inviting Senator Edward Kennedy to be honored.

"People didn't think he would come. I was told at that time he gets hundreds of requests a day to appear some place. Governor Mandel told me to try by offering him 30 different dates to choose from. He not only came but drove himself over."

Although the Senator arrived somewhat late, he not only apologized, but told Leonard he would therefore stay as long as needed to sign autographs. Leonard observed that during the meal, Kennedy put a metal detector in front of himself.

That dinner proved highly successful. But Leonard then decided to pursue an even bigger attraction, especially for a Jewish organization. He wanted Henry Kissinger—the first Jewish Secretary of State—to come to Chizuk Amuno to accept its Distinguished Leadership Award.

In a display of his commitment and drive to achieve his goals, Leonard began by approaching Maryland's two United States senators at the time: Charles M.C. Mathias, Jr., and J. Glenn Beall, Jr.. He had arranged for the two of them to be honored together at Chizuk Amuno the year before, with New York's Senator Jacob Javits as featured speaker. He asked them to encourage Kissinger to accept the brotherhood's invitation. He also sought support from several congressmen, Governor Mandel, and Senator Javits to seek Secretary

Kissinger's acceptance.

Eventually, Secretary Kissinger agreed, and on Sunday, May 9, 1976—Mother's Day—he attended the Chizuk Amuno Brotherhood Donor Dinner as its honored guest. Soon after his arrival, he told Leonard "both of Maryland's senators were very insistent I come here tonight."

Kissinger's appearance at Chizuk Amuno, which had been heralded several weeks before with announcement on the cover of the Baltimore Jewish Times, was special in several ways. It was soon obvious that Kissinger regarded this as a meaningful evening for him. He brought his wife, and the two of them showed interest in Leonard and Phyllis. In fact, Kissinger's staff had researched Leonard's life for the Secretary, and he knew about the Attman family. He also thanked Leonard for inviting his parents, who could not come but who, said Kissinger, "would have been proud." The President sent a telegram congratulating him on his honor. And Kissinger's wife confided that night to Phyllis that this was the first time that her husband had agreed to speak at a synagogue after being appointed Secretary of State. Leonard thinks that this also may have been the only time Kissinger spoke in a synagogue while Secretary of State.

The evening was a stunning success. More than 1800 people attended, so many that a tent had to be erected adjacent to the synagogue to accommodate everyone. Non-Jews as well as Jews were in the audience, including, as the Jewish Times reported, "prominent religious, judicial, and political officials from Maryland, the District of Columbia, and the United States Government." Security was extremely tight, with the secret service locking down the building once the program started. Kissinger, says Leonard, "was very gracious, shook hands, and allowed us to take him through the tent so everyone could see him."

Leonard also had a chance to talk with Secretary Kissinger. Two things he said have remained with Leonard.

"He told me that as Secretary of State, his belief was that 'I want to keep people talking and then you don't have war.'"

Then, sometime that evening, Kissinger, who knew about Leonard's successful business career, asked him a question that was revealing for what it said about the differences in experience for the German-born Kissinger and the American-born Attman. Asked Secretary Kissinger, "How do the banks treat you as a Jew?"

Taken somewhat aback by the question, Leonard responded by telling him how his father had always taught him and his brothers that "whatever money you make is merely a loan, that you are only a temporary trustee of it to do good things with." Leonard said that whenever he went to a bank for a loan or an extension, he would recount this story to a banker, and invariably received a favorable reception.

How does one person have the time and energy to do so much for so many, to be able to attend to his own work while working to raise money and orchestrate events for others?

When asked that question, Leonard answers, "I guess there's that old saying that if you want to get something done, give it to a busy person." He then adds, "It is difficult to turn down a good cause."

Leonard says he looks for a key component in the charities and causes with which he becomes involved. "You look to see if there is in the people in the organization a passion for the cause. No one person can make any event a success by himself. You have to have the team of people and the passion there. You can tell if there is enough of a passion there to make the project a success."

Leonard has shown that he himself has that passion for that "good cause." Blending business with philanthropy, work with civic endeavors: this has been Leonard's guiding principle and passion.

This same passion for excelling in one's pursuits while doing for others can also be seen in the lives of Leonard's brothers and their families. This may be why he and the other Attmans have built not only successful companies, but what Leonard's father and mother prized: a good name.

Chapter Seven

FROM GENERATION TO GENERATION: CARRYING THE ATTMAN NAME FURTHER

"It's Attmansphere!"

— Stuart Attman, a third-generation Attman, created this term for the special family feeling in the deli and among the Attmans

It is the second night of Passover in 2011 and the Attmans are gathered for their annual family Seder. But this is not the usual small family affair. Here, grouped around seven large tables, are four generations of Attmans—more than 60 people now—the descendants of Harry and Ida, the progeny of Edward, Leonard, and Seymour and their spouses. Here are Attman children, their children's children, and even great-grandchildren. Here are nieces, nephews, and cousins, even 6th cousins ("how many people can say they know and see their sixth cousins?" notes a fourth-generation Attman).

Gary and Ron conduct the Seder and keep the proceedings moving at a lively pace. To ask 'The Four Questions' that start the proceedings, they call on the children of what is now the fifth generation of Attmans in America—the great-great-grand children of Harry and Ida. As of 2012, this totaled eleven youngsters. Then, it's time for reciting the Hagaddah, and family members from around the room read a portion. The atmosphere is jovial and the youngest children are kept engaged through a variety of tried and true techniques, including songs, coloring books, plastic frogs, and other props and kid-friendly food. As the evening proceeds, the focus for the young becomes finding the Afikomen, the broken piece of hidden matzoh that once located will serve as the Seder's dessert. With so many looking, the older Attmans have arranged to have six to eight pieces scattered around the room. One young Attman says the adults usually hide the Afikomen in the room's piano, another says a key spot has been under the couch. Once found, the matzohs are presented to the grandparents for prizes.

In the early days of the growing family, the Attmans did not have one large Seder, but over time the family patriarchs began to feel that Passover offered an opportunity to gather together. The celebration of a family-wide Seder began in earnest in the mid-1970s and was held in different homes and locations, but with the continued growth of the family the decision was made in the mid-1990s to move the second Seder to the large boardroom at the Woodholme Country Club. What is remarkable, however, is not just the size of the group at these festive holiday meals. It is the closeness exhibited, the sense of unity expressed of something they each hold very dear—being an Attman.

"It's a beautiful scene to see, to sit down, share a meal and share a common lineage. It's a wonderful way to maintain relationships," says one of the third generation of Attmans. "Our parents did not want us to become too insular from each other. Here cousins of the same age who might not meet all year get to come together."

Says another Attman, "It's good to see our growing family at a Seder, not like many other families who only seem to see each other at funerals."

In keeping with the openness of the Attmans, everyone knows he or she could also bring to the Seder a non-family friend, whether Jewish or not.

Jessica, Eileen's daughter and one of Seymour's three granddaughters, now lives in New Jersey. She recounts how her husband, Evan, who is from New Jersey, was "overwhelmed by the size of the family" when he came to his first Attman Seder. He also expressed amazement at learning how much of her family resides so close together in Baltimore, remarking, "Your family lives within a five mile radius!"

Indeed, the Attmans exhibit both a physical and emotional closeness. At one time Ed, Leonard and Seymour lived on the same block, as did Harry Attman. On the Jewish High Holidays, the three brothers, along with some of their children and their families, always sat in the same rows in Chizuk Amuno. At lunchtime at Acme Paper, one can find Ed, along with three sons and four grandchildren who work there, having lunch together at a restaurant near the company's headquarters. Steven's son Michael, who is the youngest Attman working at Acme, marvels at "going out to lunch every day with my grandfather, my dad, two of my uncles, and three cousins. It's an amazing experience! "

As previously mentioned, Leonard's daughters Shellye and Wende work with him in his various real estate operations, son Jeffrey in both real estate and healthcare, and nephew Gary in FutureCare. Jeffrey's son Jonathan, as a sophomore at the University of Alabama, interned in the summer with his grandfather Leonard, getting first-hand business and management experience and involvement with Leonard's charitable causes. As Leonard points out, "This adds another dimension and extension of family in our business and brings in a fourth generation."

In 2001, three generations of Attmans, including cousins, traveled together to Tampa, Florida, to see the Baltimore Ravens play in the Super Bowl. They also witnessed together the University of Maryland's NCAA final victory in Atlanta in 2002. In 2013, more than 25 family members attended that year's Super Bowl in New Orleans to root for the Ravens in their surprising victory. Says Scott Attman of this and similar family experiences, "We Attmans travel in packs."

The physical closeness comes out of an emotional tug created as far back as when Harry married Ida, for the both of them were warm personalities who demonstrated the importance of family to their three sons, who then conveyed that to their children and later generations.

Shellye notes how her Uncle Edward is "warm to all of us" and "never made me feel like just a niece." Lisa, Ed's granddaughter, spoke in the same way about her granduncle Leonard, who when he traveled to New York City would frequently contact her and take her to dinner while she was living and studying in New York. Gary, Ed's son, refers to his working relationship with his Uncle Leonard as one in which he feels Leonard is "not just my uncle but my confidante and friend."

And Seymour's grandchildren remember him with fondness for his caring ways. Marc's daughter, Alison, still recalls how her grandfather took her and his grandniece Jessica on shopping trips to Washington, DC. She also cherishes the time when she had just given birth to her first child, Samuel (named for her late uncle Stuart). Her grandfather, who could no longer drive, called a taxi and showed up in her room. "I couldn't believe it; my parents used to drive him everywhere and here he called a cab himself; it was so nice." Alison and her husband, Ronald, named their second child Sarah, for Seymour. Their third child, Ava, is named for her grandmother and Seymour's first wife, Ruth.

Says Jessica of Seymour, "He was there for me, emotionally and financially. He made sure I went to Hebrew school and summer camp. Later he was proud of me when I became independent in my career and, without asking, paid for an expensive briefcase for my job."

Over the years, cousins Alison and Jessica, although they now live in different states (Florida and New Jersey), have kept in close contact. "We talk by phone every day," says Alison. "We've always been close together, even as little girls."

Indeed, all the cousins stay in touch through Facebook and other social media.

Eileen's daughter Chelsea worked summers with Ed at Acme Paper. She was very young when her grandfather Seymour died, but still remembers him as "a highly respected man" and someone who "commanded the attention of everyone in the room." She vividly recalls his attentiveness to family: "He was loving and endearing and giving, and he cared about his family more than anything in the world. He would do anything for the people he loved."

When asked what makes for a typical Attman family member, many of the Attmans responded the same: understanding the importance of family. Steven points out that at a time today when the members of many families are distant, often split apart by indifference or jealousies, the Attmans, thanks in large part to what Harry and Ida instilled in their children and children's children, are close and supportive.

"We have a tremendous devotion to family and to family values," says Shellye. "We have a genuine concern for each other. That's why we call what we do at work 'a family business' and not 'a business family'."

The younger generations of Attmans are also following very much in another Attman path—a commitment to community. One can find third and fourth generation Attmans serving in leadership roles or as active committee members or by volunteering to raise funds for a wide variety of organizations helping diverse populations. They are involved with college campus organizations ... non-profit summer camps ... synagogues ... day schools ... PTAs ... Israel... young professional groups...Jewish federation committees... Maryland's higher education system ... student associations ... community arts programs ... social organizations ... playgrounds for the underprivileged ... an orphanage in the Dominican Republic ... a social service program on Native American reservations.

Shellye served as chair of the Women's Division, State of Israel Bonds, of Maryland and is very involved in the Beth Tfiloh Congregation. To raise funds for the Beth Tfiloh Community Day School, she headed a committee of 200 women who created a cookbook that has brought in thousands of dollars (called *America Cooks Kosher*, the book, which features 320 recipes including Bubbe Attman's famous honey cake recipe, sells for $30 at selected bookstores as well as online at www.bethtfiloh.com/cookbook). She has also served as chair of Spotlight, Beth Tfiloh Day School's major annual fund raiser. Since 1990, she has been involved in the Jemicy School, which her parents helped found.

Ron has been president of the Bonnie View Country Club and vice president of Jewish Community Services. Ron and his wife, Stephanie, served in 2012 as co-chairs of what was the largest one-night fundraising event in Maryland—the LifeBridge Magic of Life Gala, which raised close to $3 million for LifeBridge Health, a regional health care system operating hospitals, nursing homes and medical offices.

Steven, along with Leonard, serves on the executive board of Shoresh, an outreach organization with a camp in Frederick County that seeks to build a positive Jewish identity for youngsters and their families regardless of affiliation or observance. Steven also served as secretary of the Executive Board of Beth Tfiloh from 2004 to 2006, and twice was corporate chair for Beth Tfiloh's Spotlight event—in 2000 when Dionne Warwick performed and in 2005 when Jay Leno starred, raising monies for the day school's scholarship fund.

Like many of the younger generation of Attmans, Gary is a graduate of the University of Maryland. He also graduated from the University's Law School. Among his community activities, Gary has served as president of the Chizuk Amuno Congregation, a leader in the Conservative Jewish movement with more than 1300-member families. Additionally, in 2009, the Governor of Maryland named him to the University's Board of Regents, a highly important position in the state's educational system. As a regent, he helps oversee the operations of all of the institutions of higher learning that are part of the state's university system. Along with other regents, he has responsibility for an annual budget that runs in the billions of dollars and the education of tens of thousands of students.

When Gary was sworn in along with other gubernatorial appointees at a ceremony in the State House, Maryland's Secretary of State John McDonough told him that as a matter of protocol he was to sign a book (Gary says it "was enormous and looked like the Guttenberg Bible") that contained the signatures of all appointees to various state boards over the years. He was then shown that, underneath the line for his signature, was another line. This line, he was told, was optional, but his signature here was to affirm his belief in God.

An observant Jew, Gary vividly remembers the scene. "I thought for a moment about my college days, that as a student at UM I had never met the university's president, yet the week before my swearing-in I had been invited to have lunch with the university's president and his vice-presidents. I thought about all this and that here I was, a third generation Attman, being sworn in by the Governor himself as a regent for the State of Maryland's university system, I said to myself, 'Yes, there is a God!', and signed my name."

Fourth generation Attmans are present in the workings of the Jewish Community Center, which serves the athletic and cultural needs of all ages...the Jewish Federation of Baltimore's Impact Events Committee, geared to bringing young Jewish adults together socially...and the Federation's Young Business Roundtable Committee and Young Leadership program, which work to interest young people to become involved in the organization's charitable work.

Ron's daughter Lisa, before giving birth, was director of Kaboom, a non-profit, organization which raises funds and enlists volunteers to build hundreds of playgrounds in underprivileged areas of cities nationwide. Ron's twin sons, Andy and Keith, are active in leadership roles in various Federation agency boards. Gary's daughter Sarah, as a high school student, organized the first Jewish Student Association at Bryn Mawr High School in Roland Park, and daughter Carly, when in college, spent summers working with Jewish artists in a community-based public art program in West Baltimore entitled "Rebuilding Through Art Project."

In a symbolic connection between the generations, Leonard and

Phyllis's granddaughter, Marissa, became the University of Maryland's Jewish Student Life Coordinator at the University's Hillel Center, which annually serves several thousand Jewish college students (22 percent of UM students are Jewish) and is one of the largest of Hillels providing for Jewish college students on numerous campuses around the country. It was at this Hillel that Leonard and Phyllis first met. More than half a century later, Marissa headed Hillel's Tzedek Program, which oversees Hillel's community service, social justice and advocacy efforts. She later went on to work in development for the Jewish Social Services Association of Washington, D.C..

Among Leonard's other grandchildren can be seen unusual involvement in school and community. Harris Levitas (the son of daughter, Wende, and her husband Michael) performs community service in various nursing homes; Erin Levitas has volunteered at the Ronald McDonald House and raised funds for cancer research by participating in dance and race marathons.

Jeffrey's children—Nicole, Jonathan, and Matthew—have exhibited accomplishments in a range of activities. Nicole was a competitive figure skater through early adolescence, was elected president of her middle school, and was inducted into two honor societies in college. Her goal is to be a school psychologist. Jonathan, in high school, distinguished himself both in the classroom and on the athletic field: his high GPA earned him a four year honor student status, dean's list, and an alumni award. In college, he was inducted into the National Honor Society for his high GPA and placement on the dean's list. Matthew, the youngest of the three, has shown in high school that he is a skillful musician, with multiple talents for the stage and for technical work behind the scenes. He wants to make a career in entertainment.

This brief survey bears out what Ron's son Scott has said about his generation of Attmans, how they have always been instilled with a "sense of responsibility to community, to selves and to others." There has been, too, the transmission, as Shellye has said, of "helping the world at large." And that sense has come through in the examples set by Harry and Ida's three sons.

"The apple doesn't fall far from the Grandpa's tree!" Shellye once said about Leonard's grandchildren. The same could be said about the other Attman children and grandchildren, as well as about the three brothers themselves—all of whom are now carrying forward the fruit of Harry and Ida's tree.

The Attman name has come to have a special resonance for others. This is largely due to the continued existence of the Lombard Street delicatessen and the enticing culinary memories the store has aroused in generations of patrons. But the widespread recognition of the Attmans is also undoubtedly due to the positive image its members have made over four generations in the life and times of their communities. When he was alive, Stuart Attman, who worked closely with his dad, Seymour, in the delicatessen, coined a term for the family spirit in and outside of the deli: he called it 'Attmansphere.'

And that Attmansphere has helped make the name and family widely known, not only in Baltimore but elsewhere. Alison sees it in Florida, where anyone with origins from the East Coast, once learning her maiden name is Attman, will ask if she is an Attman from the delicatessen and, if so, "which one are you?"

Ron's wife, Stephanie, relates that when ordering an item by phone from a company based in California, she mentioned she was calling from Baltimore and her last name was Attman. The sales person asked if she was related to the delicatessen people. "That happens all the time," she says. "It's like being a celebrity. Everywhere we go, people recognize the name and get excited about the deli."

Chelsea says she "does not think more than a month goes by in my life when I don't meet someone who knows about the deli. Someone always knows someone who had Attman's cater their Bar Mitzvah or who goes to the store every Sunday before a Ravens game or heard about us from their husband's nephew's Hebrew school teacher and goes every time they're in Baltimore and won't order corned beef anywhere else."

Gary's daughter Sarah recounts how "when I was a little girl, my dad made it pretty clear that my last name was something to be proud of. To this day when I walk around Baltimore and someone learns I'm an Attman, their face brightens. They know my father, my mother, my cousin, my Zadey. They always know an Attman and it's someone they love. In high school, everyone was impressed that my family owned that deli. I'd brag about it, acting like I went downtown to order corned beef on rye almost every other day." To Sarah, being an Attman means "you are a member of a strong Baltimore family."

Carly, Gary's other daughter, says that "to our family, material things and money are secondary to connections between people." She points to a conversation she had with her grandfather, Ed, after she had returned from a trip to China and "was bragging to him about how she bargained with everyone who tried to sell her something." She said that, with a crowd looking on to see who would back down first, she was able to "haggle down" a man trying to sell her a sweet potato at twice the regular price, but succeeded in winding up with the usual price. When she finished her story, her grandfather gently admonished her for the hardcore bargaining. She immediately realized his message. What she learned from her grandfather, she said, was "if you have money, use it. Use it to take care of yourself, buy yourself something nice. But also, and absolutely more importantly, take care of someone else. Pay for those who can't pay." She realized then, she said, that "my bargaining battle was all about pride. I didn't want to be taken for advantage. Zayde would forget all about his pride. He's confident in doing the right thing."

"I'm so appreciative of the Attman family," says Carly. "I've got stability. I feel safe and cared for. There's tradition and bond here. And the man at the helm has a heart of platinum."

Ron has seen the deli's popularity enhance other areas in which family members are involved. "The deli is a good 'door opener' for us at Acme Paper. People know and love the place." And Acme sales people will bring clients to the delicatessen for a business lunch. Leonard, too, has seen how the Attman name has facilitated his many business dealings and civic efforts. Gary notes that when he goes "to Annapolis, Glen Burnie, or Towson" he finds a receptive audience "because they know my relationship to the store."

Attman's Delicatessen is also well-known because the brothers Ed, Seymour, and Leonard and now Marc are themselves well-known, with many friends. And, then, too there are the many influential politicians, business executives, and professional people, as well as laborers and a wide swath of Baltimoreans of all backgrounds who have frequented the deli over the decades and told others. Propelling that attraction is that the store, with its aromas, extensive menu, range of delicacies, and jaunty banter between employees and patrons, has created its own beloved personality. Here is where individuals can come together to enjoy a haven of comfort food in a warm, welcoming atmosphere. Gary's wife Patricia, a physician, remembers first learning about Attman's Delicatessen while rotating through nearby Johns Hopkins and University of Maryland hospitals during her medical school and residency years. "It was the only nourishment fit for rejuvenation after hours and hours on call," she recalls. "There, we medical doctors bonded and shared clinical information. We may have even saved a few lives by our discussions over lunch at Attman's deli."

Today, Attman's Delicatessen on Lombard Street, a fixture in East Baltimore for nearly a century, is one of the sole survivors of the many shops in a once-crowded heart of Jewish Baltimore. It is also one of the few thriving delis of a dwindling number nationwide (New York City, the mecca for Jewish delis, at one point offered 2000; today, that city has only 25). The store has had an impact far beyond its narrow confines and its modest beginnings. From what Harry and Ida began and what has been built upon by their sons, along with their spouses and children, has emerged major business successes in a variety of fields, employing and serving thousands of people. From it has come stunning contributions to the economic, civic, religious, and philanthropic life of Maryland. And from it has come a story of how strong family values can be created, transmitted, and sustained over generations.

As Steven has pointed out, what Harry and Ida created has been akin to "the tree that gives food and shade so that its seedlings can do the same." The result, he notes, is the Biblical blessing that "the seeds you give off will be as beautiful and plentiful as you are."

"My grandparents never went on a plane and had few desires, just worked for their children," Steven says. "And their three children are true personalities of their own. They each have their own charisma, set of friends, and way of doing business. They are all driven in different ways and have their own vision, and yet they work in harmony. Each one could be a patriarch of the entire family. It's like we have three pillars on which to build."

Responding to a question about what it means to be a member of the Attman family, Chelsea, among the youngest of the current generation of Attmans, wrote: "To be a part of the Attman family means you are a part of history, a part of tradition. Because of the hard work of my grandfather and my great-grandfather, 'Attman' is now a Jewish household name. I am humbled at the thought of how much my family has accomplished."

Rabbi David Finkelstein, who has known the Attmans since he taught Steven's son Michael his Bar Mitvah in 1997 and who spoke at the shiva house when David's wife, Bobbie, died, is also impressed with how family members treat others. "They will do anything to help somebody. They can't run fast enough to do good."

The response of the community to the breadth of Attman giving could be seen within a two-week span in May-June 2010 when first a camp and then a day school celebrated Attman family support.

On May 23, Camp Shoresh's pavilion was filled to capacity—with even Ravens football players in attendance at an annual barbecue—as the camp presented Edward and Mildred and their family with a large white cake decorated with thanks for their involvement. [Mildred passed away two years later at the age of 89. She and Edward had been married 66 years.]

On June 3, every seat in Beth Tfiloh's large sanctuary was filled, as more than 1400 people, including major political figures, donors, students, and parents came to honor Leonard and Phyllis for their many years of service and substantial contributions to Beth Tfiloh and its day school. With acclaimed musician and Broadway performer Michael Cavanaugh providing a rousing evening of entertainment (at times the audience joined in, clapping to the music, and students danced in the aisles), the event raised more than $750,000 from individual and corporate sponsors. This was among the largest sums donated in the history of the school's Spotlight events, enabling Lennie to fulfill the goal he expressed in his speech that evening of "helping Jewish education and promoting Jewish spirituality."

Helping make possible summers of religious and spiritual experiences for Jewish youth... raising funds for schooling steeped in Jewish values and knowledge—the sons of Harry and Ida have carried on a mission and a tradition started by their parents. And now, as seen in this chapter, in the best evidence that lessons have been learned and absorbed, the story of the Attman family is still unfolding, as the next generations following Edward, Seymour and Leonard are making their mark and carrying the Attman name further.

The striking aspect of this multi-generational story of the Attman family is how it has all emanated from two young people new to America and without funds, who as recent newlyweds began a modest little enterprise in a poor section of Baltimore in the first decades of the previous century. But Harry and Ida possessed something more meaningful than money. They possessed a combination of the values of hard work (to paraphrase Harry, "Sell every day or you're a bum"), ethics (treat customers fairly, even giving proper change in a customer's language), and a religious tradition of being mindful about the needs of others (responding readily with charity and, if needed, food for the poor). They showed that the best way to conduct a business day-to-day was to earn customer loyalty that would endure year-to-year. They built their business on these virtues in a manner that resulted in more than a way to make a living. It resulted in a way to make a life: for them and their progeny. Theirs was a vision for building—both business and family—for the future.

Indeed, Harry and Ida's greatest contribution was their ability to impart all these values to their children Edward, Seymour, and Leonard and now, through them, to future generations of Attmans. As Steven's daughter Rachel wrote, "My great-grandparents left us a wonderful legacy. I thank God for that."

This remarkable legacy may have been best captured in a statement made during one of the interviews for this book. Ron had been providing an overview of the family's multi-generational history, the many businesses spawned, and the Attmans' wide-ranging involvement in numerous civic and charitable causes. Ron soon paused and thought a moment. He then remarked, almost in disbelief himself, "And just think, it all started with a deli."

Attman's Delicatessen continues to show vitality.

In 2006, it opened the largest concession stand in M&T Bank Stadium where the Baltimore Ravens play. In 2013, Attman's opened another full-service location—a 4,000 sq.ft. delicatessen/restaurant in Potomac, Md., serving breakfast, lunch, and dinner, along with catering, seven days a week.

The new location, near the D.C. metro area, is nearly twice the size of Attman's on Lombard Street, which continues in operations as it has for nearly a century.

The Attman Family Tree (as of April 1, 2013)

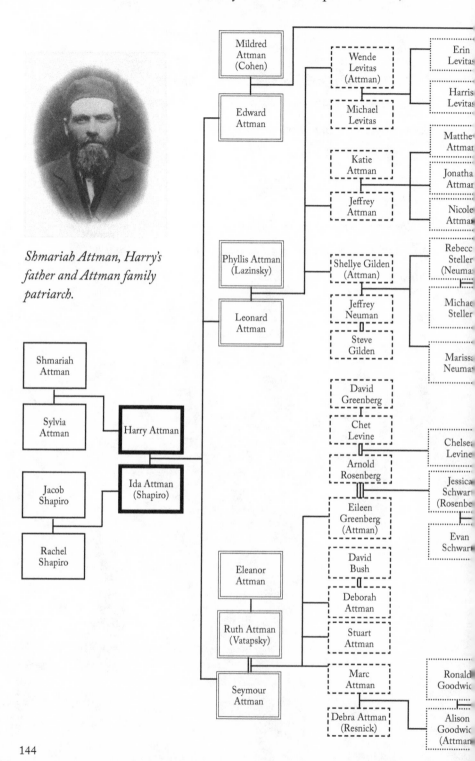

Shmariah Attman, Harry's father and Attman family patriarch.

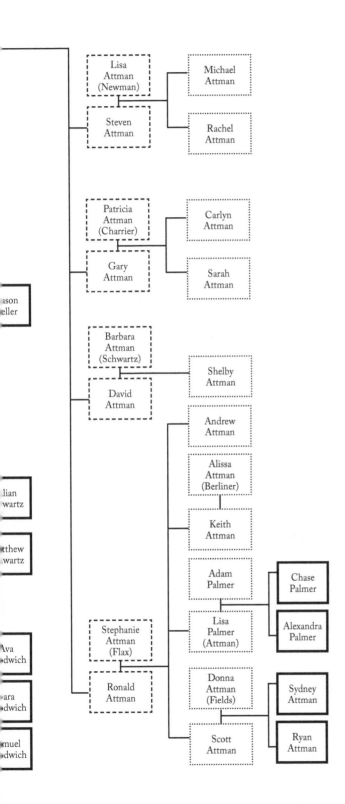

PHOTO SECTION

Deli and Family History
Various Attman Businesses
Civic and Charitable Activities
The Present Generation

Harry and Ida Attman, founders of Attman's Delicatessen, sit for a
picture taken during their wedding year in 1918. Harry was 25 and
Ida was 18.

The front of today's Attman's Delicatessen at 1019 East Lombard Street, on what has been called "Baltimore's Corned Beef Row."

The interior of Attman's Kibbitz Room, first introduced by Seymour Attman, son of the founder.

Lombard Street during the 1920s.

Lombard Street during the 1950s.

The First Family: Left to right: (Seated) Ida and Harry Attman.
(Standing) Phyllis, Leonard, Edward, Mildred, Ruth and Seymour
Attman.

No. 17001   3 Class

SWEDISH AMERICAN LINE

PREPAID TICKET RECEIPT

to be kept by the purchaser

Agency at _Baty Md_

Date _2/14/21_

Names of Passengers		Adult age	Child age	Inf. age
Schwarja	Gellma	48		
Blume	"	55		
Ruchel	"	24		
Joseph	"	~2		
Jocha	"	20		
Reuben	"	18		
Rizze	"	16		
Solomon	"	13		
Chaika	"		9	
Annie	"		6	
Passenger's post office address				

Total Number of Passengers   8   2

Received from _Harry Attman_

the amount of $ _1471.00_

as passage-money for the persons named above

in the _Third_ class of one of the steamers of

SWEDISH AMERICAN LINE

from _Hamburg_

to NEW YORK

and _Balt Md_ class transportation

from New York to _Balta Md_

Amount paid for Ocean Fare   - $ _1125.00_

do.   do.   American R. R. Fare $ _65.16_

do.   do.   U. S. Head Tax   - $ _56.00_

Landing money $ _225.00_

              $1471.16

H Blaustein   Agent.

☞ SEE OTHER SIDE.

This is the receipt showing how much Harry Attman paid to bring to America 10 members of his family in 1921. The total was $1,471, a very large sum in those days and one that Harry had to borrow. It took him years to pay it back.

153

Leonard   Seymour   Edward

The Attman brothers together. (Left to right) Leonard, Seymour and Edward.

Ida and Harry stroll along Baltimore Street near Charles Street in downtown Baltimore during the 1940s. On the left is their youngest son, 10-year-old Leonard.

Seymour Attman stands beside an early sign touting the deli's corned beef sandwiches—and price.

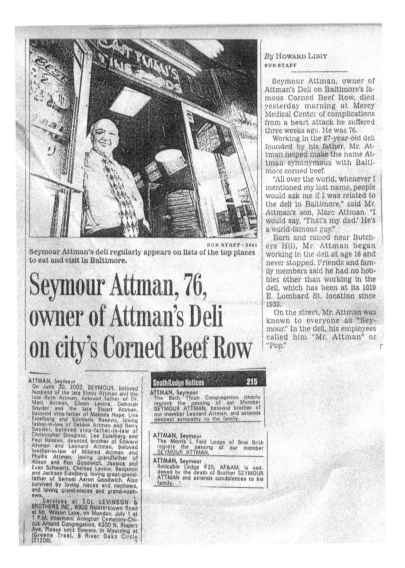

Seymour Attman, owner of Attman's Deli on Baltimore's famous Corned Beef Row, died yesterday morning at Mercy Medical Center of complications from a heart attack he suffered three weeks ago. He was 76.

Working in the 87-year-old deli founded by his father, Mr. Attman helped make the name Attman synonymous with Baltimore corned beef.

"All over the world, whenever I mentioned my last name, people would ask me if I was related to the deli in Baltimore," said Mr. Attman's son, Marc Attman. "I would say, 'That's my dad.' He's a world-famous guy."

Born and raised near Butchers Hill, Mr. Attman began working in the deli at age 16 and never stopped. Friends and family members said he had no hobbies other than working in the deli, which has been at its 1019 E. Lombard St. location since 1933.

On the street, Mr. Attman was known to everyone as "Seymour." In the deli, his employees called him "Mr. Attman" or "Pop."

Seymour Attman's deli regularly appears on lists of the top places to eat and visit in Baltimore.

Seymour Attman, 76, owner of Attman's Deli on city's Corned Beef Row

ATTMAN, Seymour
On June 30, 2002, SEYMOUR, beloved husband of the late Elinor Attman and the late Ruth Attman, beloved father of Dr. Marc Attman, Eileen Levine, Deborah Snyder and the late Stuart Attman, beloved step-father of Melinda Hope, Lisa Eidelberg and Kimberly Rasevic, loving father-in-law of Debbie Attman and Barry Snyder, beloved step-father-in-law of Christopher Douglass, Lee Eidelberg and Paul Rasevic, devoted brother of Edward Attman and Leonard Attman, beloved brother-in-law of Mildred Attman and Phyllis Attman, loving grandfather of Alison and Ron Goodwich, Jessica and Evan Schwartz, Chelsea Levine, Benjamin and Jackson Eidelberg, loving great-grand-father of Samuel Aaron Goodwich. Also survived by loving nieces and nephews, and loving grand-nieces and grand-nephews.
Services at SOL LEVINSON & BROTHERS INC., 8900 Reisterstown Road at Mt. Wilson Lane, on Monday, July 1 at 1 P.M. Interment Arlington Cemetery-Chizuk Amuno Congregation, 4300 N. Rogers Ave. Please omit flowers. In Mourning at (Greene Tree), 8 River Oaks Circle (21208).

Death/Lodge Notices 215

ATTMAN, Seymour
The Beth Tfiloh Congregation deeply regrets the passing of our Member SEYMOUR ATTMAN, beloved brother of our member Leonard Attman, and extends deepest sympathy to the family.

ATTMAN, Seymour
The Morris I. Feld Lodge of Bnai Brith regrets the passing of our member SEYMOUR ATTMAN.

ATTMAN, Seymour
Amicable Lodge #25, AF&AM, is saddened by the death of Brother SEYMOUR ATTMAN and extends condolences to his family.

When Seymour died, The Sun published an extensive and endearing obituary.

Street naming: Then-Mayor Martin O'Malley dedicates a street near the Deli in memory of Seymour Attman. Left to right: Deborah, Eileen, Chelsea, Samuel, Marc, and Debra Attman; Earl Oppel, deli manager; State Senator Nathaniel McFadden; Mayor O'Malley; Councilwoman Rikki Spector; then-Congressman Ben Cardin, and Edward Attman. Photo by Jay L. Baker, Office of the Mayor

Stuart Attman , who was very involved in the operation of the delicatessen with his father Seymour, passed away in 1994 in an accidental drowning while on vacation in Jamaica. Termed "the mayor of Lombard Street" for his vivacious personality, he was 34 years old.

This garage served in 1946 as the first base of operations for Edward's Acme Paper & Supply Co.

Acme Paper, which started with just Edward and Mildred, grew to
become a major supplier of thousands of paper and plastic products
as well as kitchen and restaurant equipment and hundreds of other
small and large items, with customers ranging from neighborhood
stores to major league stadiums, the federal government, and
Amtrak. Here Edward (center) and his sons (left to right) Steven,
David and Ronald are shown with Acme's staff in front of the
company's present office/warehouse complex built in Savage,
Maryland, in 1979. This photo was taken in 1996 on Acme's 50th
anniversary. Today, Acme has more than 250 employees.

An Attman Seder involves a number of tables as the extended Attman family comes together for the holiday. Here is Seymour's side of the family, headed by his son Marc. Shown starting from the right to left: (Standing) Dr. Marc Attman, Debra Attman, Alison Attman Goodwich, Deborah Attman, David Greenberg, Jessica Schwartz, and Evan Schwartz. (Seated) Eileen Attman Greenberg, Rebecca Greenberg, Ian Greenberg, Heather Greenberg, and Chelsea Levine.

When Leonard Attman assumed the chairmanship of the Chizuk
Amuno Congregation Brotherhood Donor Dinner in the 1960s,
he significantly increased the amount of charitable funds raised
by establishing "Cavalcade of Stars" and bringing in big name
entertainers. Here famed comedian Jimmy Durante is shown
being given the key to the city by Baltimore Mayor (and former
Governor) Theodore R. McKeldin during one such event. (Left to
right) Leonard, Jack Luskin, Jimmy Durante, Mayor McKeldin,
Joseph Lazinsky, and Harry Attman.

Leonard Attman with then-Secretary of State Henry Kissinger when Leonard, as chairman, arranged for him to be honored guest speaker at Chizuk Amuno Brotherhood Donor Dinner. This was the first and possibly only time that Kissinger, as Secretary of State, spoke in a synagogue. (Left to right) Edward Attman, Secretary Kissinger, Leonard Attman and Seymour Attman.

This is the last photo of Harry Attman with his sons. The occasion was Harry's 75th birthday, celebrated on October 25, 1968, at a Sunday morning breakfast held in his honor at Chizuk Amuno Congregation. Seated (left to right) are Edward and Harry. Standing (left to right) are Leonard and Seymour.

When Oprah came to Baltimore as the featured speaker at a Beth
Tfiloh Dahan Community School Spotlight event to raise funds
for education, she took time for a private get-together where she
asked for a tray of her favorite food from her Baltimore days—deli
from Attman's Delicatessen. Shown with her, left to right, are
Wende Attman Levitas, her daughter Erin, and Phyllis and Leonard
Attman.

Edward (left) and Leonard (right) pose with President George W. Bush when he visited Baltimore as president in May, 2006.

The former First Lady Hillary Clinton is shown in 2008 with Leonard and Phyllis when Mrs. Clinton traveled to Baltimore for a private dinner.

Governor O'Malley helps light the menorah donated by Leonard and Phyllis Attman to Government House to be used during the Governor's annual Chanukah Party co-hosted with Leonard and Phyllis, along with other members of the Attmans.

(Left to right) Gov. O'Malley, Leonard and Phyllis Attman, Nicole, Edward, Ryan, Scott, Ronald and Gary Attman. [photo courtesy of Governor's office]

Dr. Henry Brem, Hopkins neurosurgeon (left), and Dr. Gregory Riggins, Hopkins professor of neurosurgery and oncology (right), meet with Phyllis and Leonard to acknowledge "their generous gift to the Johns Hopkins Department of Neurosurgery to provide seed-money for meningioma research." Meningiomas are tumors that grow on membranes surrounding the brain and spinal chord. Although the most common of brain tumors, they are least studied because most are benign, but not all. A personal experience with the benign form prompted the couple to jump-start research.

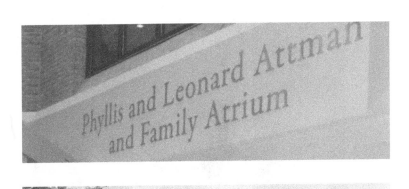

The UM Baltimore/Washington Medical Center in Anne Arundel County recognized a major donation from Phyllis and Leonard by naming the hospital's Atrium in their honor.

Edward Attman, a 1942 graduate of the University of Baltimore, and his wife, Mildred, in 2010 provided funds to establish the Edward and Mildred Cohen Attman Enterprise Hatchery in the university's Merrick School of Business. Their purpose was to establish for students a testing site for their new entrepreneurial ideas so that such concepts might one day become viable businesses. Ed said he wanted to promote in students the same spirit that enabled him to build Acme Paper & Supply from operating out of a garage to becoming an enterprise with a 3.5 million cubic ft. warehouse and six divisions handling 15,000 products. Flanking Edward and Mildred are Merrick School of Business Dean Darlene Smith and University of Baltimore President Robert Bogomolny.

In 2010, when Leonard and Phyllis were the main honorees at the
Beth Tfiloh Dahan Community School's annual Spotlight Event,
they helped raise the most money ever raised at one event for the
school's scholarship fund—more than $800,000. In recognition of
their efforts, the couple were presented with a gift of Torah scroll
handle coverings, along with a plaque engraved "for their dedication
and commitment to Jewish education and Jewish life." Left to right:
Leonard, holding their gift; Phyllis; Beth Tfiloh's Rabbi Mitchell
Wohlberg, and Mrs. Zipora Schorr, school director.

FutureCare Canton Harbor is one of 12 Baltimore area skilled nursing centers developed by FutureCare, which is owned by Leonard, Gary and Jeffrey Attman. In 2012, for the second year in a row, FutureCare was named by the Baltimore Sunpapers as number one in TopWorkplaces, based on a survey of employees in large companies in the Baltimore region. FutureCare has more than 2,500 employees.

Islands of FoxChase is the latest garden apartment complex
built and managed by Leonard Attman's real estate development
company. A Type-A luxury apartment community, it features seven
distinctive apartment floor plans and offers Islands residents a game
room with billiards, table shuffleboard, flat screen TV, kitchen, and
full-service state-of-the art gym.

Horizons is Anne Arundel County's pre-eminent professional park. With a five-story clock tower as visual focus, the 125,000 sq.ft. brick building on a 9-acre site fronting Ritchie Highway offers first floor retail space and offices on the second and third levels. Horizons is the largest and most successful retail/office commercial enterprise of Attman Properties.

The Jewish New Year in 2012 at the home of Shellye Attman
Gilden and husband Steve Gilden with their family: (Left to right,
top row) Jesse Jachman, Marissa Neuman, Jayme Gilden Wood,
Courtney Wood, Shellye Attman Gilden, Steve Gilden, Jon Gilden,
Rebecca Neuman Steller, and Michael Steller. (bottom row) Skylar
and Hayden Wood. (Not present: Mason Steller)

Fourth and fifth generations in the Attman family: Rebecca Steller
(Shellye Attman Gilden's daughter), and husband Michael Steller
with their son Mason Joseph, at 2 1/2 among the youngest of the
fifth generation of Attmans.

The next generation continues: Jeffrey Attman, son of Leonard and Phyllis, poses with his children Matthew, Nicole and Jonathan at a special family gathering.

Also present at Leonard and Phyllis's family gathering were daughter Wende Attman Levitas (second from left), her children Harris and Erin Levitas, and Wende's husband Michael.

As Steven Attman says, the Attmans travel in packs. In 2001, a number of Attmans attended together the first Ravens appearance in the Super Bowl. Shown (left to right): Scott, Lisa, Sarah, Gary, Edward, Billy Goodman (a friend), Leonard, David, Michael, Ronald and Steven Attman.

Thirty Attman family members went together to see the Ravens win the Super Bowl in 2013. Shown at BWI Airport before departure are some of the women who attended. Left to right: Wende Levitas, Marissa Neuman, Nicole Attman, Erin Levitas, Shellye Attman Gilden, Patricia Attman, and Rebecca Steller.

Ed Attman's Acme Paper & Supply Company creates and supplies many of the souvenir cups sold at Oriole Park. Here are just a sampling. Acme is a prominent provider of disposable food service supplies for stadiums throughout the Mid-Atlantic area.

Then-Orioles Ex.VP Joe Foss (center in dark suit) and Orioles player Billy Ripken, pose with six youths in Acme Paper's 'Kids at Camden' community program. The Orioles also used the occasion to congratulate Acme Paper on its 50th anniversary. Representing Acme Paper are (from right to left) Acme Paper's Jim Haire and David, Gary, Steven and Ronald Attman.

Maryland Governor Parris Glendenning presents award to Acme Paper from Restaurant Association of Maryland for Acme's outstanding service to the food service industry. Left to right: Mildred, Edward, Gov. Glendenning, Stephanie, and Ronald Attman.

Gary Attman being installed as a Regent of the University System of Maryland. (Left to right) Patricia, Gary, Governor O'Malley, Edward, David, and Lt. Gov. Brown. [Photo courtesy of the Executive Office of the Governor]

Attman family members participated in a Chizuk Amuno Congregation fund raiser for the writing of a Torah. (Standing) Left to right: Sarah, Edward, and Gary Attman. (Seated) Patricia, Carlyn and Rabbi Menachem Yulis (scribe).

50th Wedding Anniversary: Edward and Mildred Attman, who married on March 3, 1946, celebrated their 50th anniversary with their immediate family at this gathering in April, 1996. Front row (left to right): Jobi Manson and her mother Bobbie (David Attman's wife), Stephanie, Sarah, Mildred, Shelby, Michael, Edward, Carlyn, Patricia, Lisa, and Rachel. Back row (left to right): Scott, Lisa, Ronald, David, Steven, Gary, Keith, and Andrew. Except for Jobi, all last names are Attman.

Ronald and Stephanie Attman's son, Keith, great-grandson of Harry and Ida Attman, married Alissa Berliner in a ceremony in Upstate New York on June 23, 2012, nearly 100 years after Harry and Ida married. Shown relaxing after Keith and Alissa's wedding are some of the generations of Attmans born in the intervening years since Harry and Ida wed.

In July, 2013, under the direction of third-generation Marc Attman, Attman's Delicatessen expanded by opening another full-service deli, this one in Montgomery County to serve the D.C. market. Located in the Cabin John Shopping Center in Potomac, the site employs 30 people and offers the same deli fare as the Lombard Street store, with breakfast, lunch, and dinner, as well as a catering operation. At the time of the opening, 30 percent of Attman's Lombard Street business and 80 percent of its catering came from the Washington, D.C., area. As Marc told the *Baltimore Business Journal* about placing an Attman's in that market, "There are delis there, but not Attman's Deli."

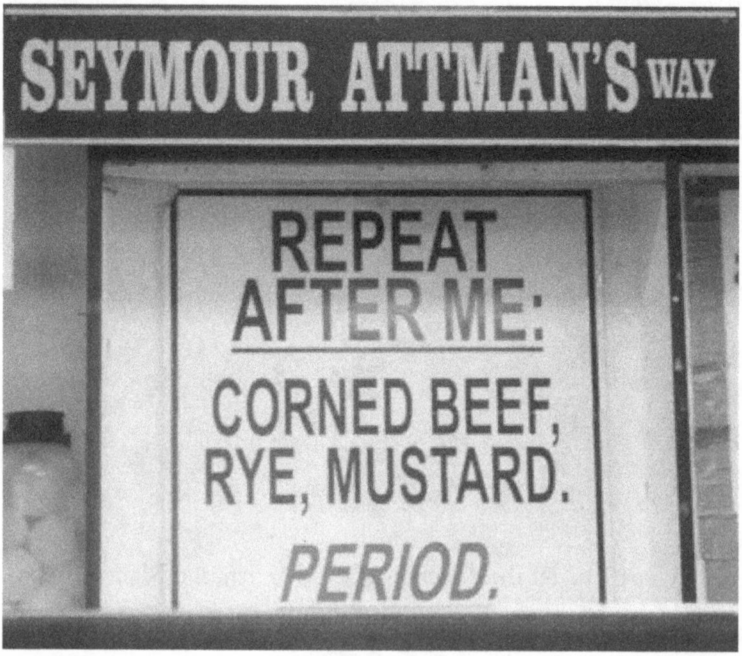
SEYMOUR ATTMAN'S WAY
REPEAT AFTER ME:
CORNED BEEF, RYE, MUSTARD.
PERIOD.

Acknowledgments

I thank the many members of the Attman family who opened their history and their hearts to me during the years I researched and wrote this book. The Attmans certainly rank as one of the most intriguing of Maryland families. This is a family who started as immigrants with literally no funds, no lodgings, no connections. Yet, as detailed in these pages, they built a beautiful, loving, caring family for themselves but also a family showing love and care for others. Their success in business and philanthropy is truly a great American success story. It is also a great human story.

I particularly wish to acknowledge several individuals within the Attman family. Ronald Attman was always there to answer questions, open doors, and arrange interviews. He helped develop the all-important Family Tree, for without it I doubt few readers would be able to locate and follow the many Attmans mentioned in this book. A number of other Attmans, notably Leonard, Edward, Gary, Marc, Steven, David, and Shellye, provided information, photos, and documents, while many others, as noted in the text, sat for interviews, answered questions or were helpful in a myriad of ways. To all of the them, I offer my appreciation.

I thank Governor Martin O'Malley for writing the Foreword. He has throughout his administrations as mayor of Baltimore and then as governor maintained close ties with the Attman family. I believe he shows here his heartfelt appreciation for the family's many civic and charitable contributions to the citizens and state of Maryland.

Others I wish to cite for various roles they played are Avi Decter, then-director of the Jewish Museum of Maryland; Dr. Robert Shapiro, a noted history and Yiddish scholar who translated for me letters in Yiddish that Harry had exchanged with his family in Europe; Gregg Wilhelm, the guiding impetus for Baltimore's book publishing scene; Jim Haire of Acme Paper; State Senator Nathaniel McFadden; Cong. C.A. Dutch Ruppersberger; Rabbi Mitchell Wohlberg; Jeffrey Reches, photographer; Barbara Federroll, executive assistant to Leonard Attman; Debra Gallo, executive assistant for FutureCare; Elaine Gershberg, Attman's catering concierge; and author and local historian Gil Sandler. My mother, Ida, who is now 103 and knew Ida Attman, contributed her memories of the family.

I also express appreciation to my wife, Gail, for her indispensable advice, constant support, and unerring grammatical and stylistic eye in the preparation of this manuscript. It is always good for an author confronting a manuscript to have a clinical psychologist available day and night.

Finally, Loyola University is to be commended for supporting a book publishing program such as Apprentice House. My particular appreciation goes to Dr. Kevin Atticks, its director and constant guide and student mentor, and to Chelsea McGuckin, the diligent creative art director on this book. For a university to provide students with real world publishing experience is worthy of a great, up-to-date university. May Apprentice House and its students and graduates flourish. And may bestsellers issue from the halls of Loyola University.

M. Hirsh Goldberg

Baltimore, Maryland — April 2013

About the Author

M. Hirsh Goldberg is a native of Baltimore and a graduate of Johns Hopkins University, with a bachelor's degree in English, a master's in teaching, and a minor in the Hopkins Creative Writing Seminars. He is accredited in public relations by the Public Relations Society of America and has headed his own PR agency, serving as consultant to many Maryland corporations and non-profit organizations.

Long involved in the local scene, he has served as press secretary and speech writer for Maryland Governor Harry Hughes and for Baltimore Mayor Theodore McKeldin. While in the mayor's office, he learned that the house in which Babe Ruth had been born was two weeks away from being destroyed by court order for being long vacant and repeatedly vandalized. He proposed the idea and initiated the successful effort to save the house and preserve it as a museum to honor Babe Ruth.

Mr. Goldberg is the author of five nationally published books, plus a special family-published volume about Maryland philanthropist Joseph Meyerhoff, and more than 450 columns, articles and Op-Ed pieces. His books have been translated into French, Chinese, Japanese and Korean. Among his writing credits, he wrote a marketing column in *The Daily Record* for two years and the Maryland Press Club twice named it the best non-daily column in a Maryland publication. He also wrote for nine years a weekly column in *The Baltimore Jewish Times* and the national Smolar Award cited the column for "excellence in Jewish journalism."

A frequent lecturer on his writings, Mr. Goldberg has been interviewed about his books on numerous local and national television and radio shows. His email address is mhgoldberg@comcast.net.

Also By the Author

The Jewish Connection

The Jewish Paradox

The Blunder Book

The Book of Lies

The Complete Book of Greed

Joseph Meyerhoff: A Portrait

Talented writers, innovative students, fresh minds at work.

Apprentice House is the country's only campus-based, student-staffed book publishing company. Directed by professors and industry professionals, it is a nonprofit activity of the Communication Department at Loyola University Maryland.

Using state-of-the-art technology and an experiential learning model of education, Apprentice House publishes books in untraditional ways. This dual responsibility as publishers and educators creates an unprecedented collaborative environment among faculty and students, while teaching tomorrow's editors, designers, and marketers.

Outside of class, progress on book projects is carried forth by the AH Book Publishing Club, a co-curricular campus organization supported by Loyola University Maryland's Office of Student Activities.

Eclectic and provocative, Apprentice House titles intend to entertain as well as spark dialogue on a variety of topics. Financial contributions to sustain the press's work are welcomed. Contributions are tax deductible to the fullest extent allowed by the IRS.

To learn more about Apprentice House books or to obtain submission guidelines, please visit www.ApprenticeHouse.com.

Apprentice House
Communication Department
Loyola University Maryland
4501 N. Charles Street
Baltimore, MD 21210
Ph: 410-617-5265 •F ax: 410-617-2198
info@apprenticehouse.com •w ww.apprenticehouse.com